D0948322

THE MARK OF CAIN

Ruth Mellinkoff

The Mark of Cain

010302

University of California Press

Berkeley • Los Angeles • London

University of California Press
Berkeley and Los Angeles, California

University of California Press, Ltd.
London, England

Library of Congress Cataloging in Publication Data

Mellinkoff, Ruth.
   The mark of Cain.

   Bibliography: p.
   Includes index.
   1. Cain. I. Title.
BS580.C3M44   222'.110924   80-18589
ISBN 0-520-03969-6

Printed in the United States of America

Contents

List of Illustrations

Preface

The biblical figure of Cain has absorbed my interest and occupied my study for a long time. As I began my investigation of the appearances of Cain in visual, literary, exegetical, and other sources, I was overwhelmed by the abundant imagery and the diverse interpretations of this evil character. For Cain's depraved humanity has served society especially well. His very "humanness" made him an excellent vehicle and scapegoat to compare with and criticize those thought to be of the same ilk; thus mankind continuously turned its kaleidoscope ever so slightly on the succinct biblical story of Cain and Abel, magnifying and splitting it into what seemed to be ever-increasing and variegated images. Slowly this massive evidence began to sort itself into smaller units and my interest and ideas began to focus on certain themes and topics, crystallizing in such a way that I realized by investigating any one of them our view of man might be enlarged. The one I have chosen for this book is the enigmatic theme of the mark of Cain.

The biblical story of Cain, tiller of the soil, and Abel, the shepherd, is a fragmentary mixture of myths; it is both incomplete and contradictory. The two brothers each bring offerings from the fruit of their toils to God. Abel's offering is accepted; Cain's is rejected; yet the biblical text says nothing about

how this was done. Cain, ignoring a divine warning
on the pitfalls of sin, then kills Abel. For this heinous
act of brother murder he is doubly punished—denied
the fruits of the soil and condemned to be a fugitive-
wanderer on earth. Yet only a few verses later Cain
founds the first city—Enoch. After the slaying of
Abel, Cain expresses fear of being killed by anyone
who might see him. Yet his need for protection is
inexplicable since presumably there are no persons
on earth other than his parents. God, however, responds to Cain's anxiety, assuring him that this will
not happen: The Lord threatens anyone who might
kill Cain with a sevenfold punishment, and that Cain
might be recognized, God places a mark of some kind
on Cain—or sets a sign for Cain.

What the mark was, and whether it was a warning
sign or a protective device, are matters of speculation.
It has lent itself to a wide range of interpretations.
Though the biblical data was insufficient for providing an explanation of Cain's peculiar mark, nevertheless, interpretations were plentifully provided. The
interpretations selected for this study come in the
main from the centuries before the Protestant Refor-
mation. It is not that post-Reformation interpretations are without interest but only that the earlier interpretations have suffered neglect at the hands of a
generation of scholars to whom "fanciful interpretation" has tended to mean "worthless interpretation."
The interpretations here studied have, precisely because of their fancy, satisfied man's desire for en-
lightenment, served a didactic purpose, and nourished
the needs of fanciful imaginations.

Discussion of the mark of Cain has occurred in so many cultures and so many humanistic disciplines that I could never have completed this study without the generous collaboration of many wonderful librarians, curators, colleagues, and friends. While I have tried to acknowledge all direct scholarly debts in footnotes, I should like to express special thanks, first and above all, to Walter Horn, whose enthusiasm for this essay in its earliest draft cheered and challenged me to its completion. I owe a debt of gratitude also to Gavin Langmuir, Peter Brown, Jonas Greenfield, Bezalel Narkiss, and Robert Benson, who read my manuscript, or parts of it, and offered their general criticism and suggestions; to Daniel Mellinkoff for calling my attention to Hermann Hesse's novel *Demian*, which I would otherwise have surely overlooked; to Carol Lanham for superb Latin and Greek translations; to Ann Hinckley, reference librarian of the UCLA Graduate Research Library, for assistance on Mormon theology; to William McClung and John Miles, both of the University of California Press, for useful and constructive suggestions in the final stages of revision; and to Regina Neuman, for efficiency in many chores of which typing is only one. Last but certainly not least, I want to express both my appreciation of, and my admiration for, David Mellinkoff, who manages to play "Devil's Advocate" and "Guardian Angel" with equal expertise.

Introduction

Modern biblical source criticism has frequently seen Cain as the eponymous ancestor of the Kenites—a nomadic clan of smiths who possibly wore their tribal mark.[1] Source criticism of that kind, however, did not concern ancient and medieval commentators; nor were they aware of possible connections between Cain and the Kenites, except perhaps in the case of the thirteenth-century Jewish cabbalistic Zohar where the connection was made, but for all the wrong reasons.[2] Though it is of importance to penetrate the scriptural text and determine its formation, yet the weaving together of different strands of ancient legends and their arrangement and emphasis by some final redactor[3] is not at stake here. What is of concern is the biblical text as it was finally fixed, for the interpretations of the mark of Cain dealt with in this study were based on that text and its later translations.[4]

Popular, customary, present-day ideas about the mark of Cain see it as a brand or stigma meant to identify, humiliate, and punish criminal Cain, yet such notions have no basis in biblical text. The laconic biblical account in Genesis 4 of Cain and Abel provides no clues as to the nature of the mark (or sign) of Cain. It is not even certain whether a mark upon Cain's person was intended. It will be recalled that after Cain killed Abel, the Lord cursed Cain and Cain then expressed fear that whoever would see him would kill him. God replied that would not happen; the Vulgate text of Genesis 4:15 states it thus:

Dixitque ei Dominus: Nequaquam ita fiet: sed omnis qui occiderit Cain, septuplum punietur. Posuitque Dominus Cain signum, ut non interficeret eum omnis qui invenisset eum.[5]

The Douay translation of the second part of this verse reads:

And the Lord set a mark upon Cain, that whosoever found him should not kill him.

The Latin verse, however, can be, and has been (as will be seen in the course of this study), translated in at least two ways depending on whether a filled-in *in* is meant to go with Cain, or with *signum,* and therefore:

1. Posuitque [in] Cain signum / signum [in] Cain, thus meaning: placed a sign on Cain; or

2. Posuitque Cain [in] signum / [in] signum Cain, thus meaning: made Cain [as] a sign.[6]

There were other meanings also attached to the phrase which will be pointed out as this study proceeds.[7] But beyond the complications created by confusion or controversy over the grammar, there is nothing in the text which describes, or even hints at, what the characteristics of the mark or sign might have been. This lack of scriptural information did not, however, prevent fertile imaginations from filling the gap with a fascinating and contradictory panorama of conjectures, reveries, legends, and questionable traditions. To review these—primarily the ancient and medieval ones—and to analyze them—mostly by means of conceptual types—is the method I have chosen for their study. Categories inevitably overlap, yet discussion by genre is, I believe, the most interesting and illuminating way to examine the disparate interpretations of the mysterious mark.

1
Cain and Repentance

Interpretations of Cain's mark or sign have sometimes turned on how Cain himself was viewed. In early Jewish thought he represented two different types: a sinner who sincerely repented and was therefore rewarded with a token of forgiveness; or the opposite, an unregenerate, unredeemable murderer whose sign advertised his shameful deed. This amazing pendulum swing of opposing views reflects differing attitudes toward the question of Cain's repentance.

Targum texts reflect both viewpoints. Though the word Targum in general means "translation" or "interpretation," it is used here as it is most generally used in scholarly studies, to refer to the Aramaic versions of the Hebrew Bible. The origin of Targums is intimately associated with the early synagogue which in those days (before the fall of Jerusalem in A.D. 70) was primarily used for the reading or reciting of Hebrew scripture.[1] Though the Jews never forgot that Hebrew was their sacred language, by this time their understanding of Hebrew had been greatly diminished by the spread of Aramaic which had become the common language of the Near East.[2] Scripture was read in Hebrew in the synagogues and this recitation was then followed by a translator who provided a kind of translation–commentary in vernacular

Aramaic to clarify the meaning of the Hebrew for the congregation. The Targums in fact have been described as lying "half-way between straightforward translation and free retelling of the biblical narrative."[3] They ultimately evolved into different Targum traditions. What remains today are only glimpses derived from the few Targum texts or fragments that have survived. Targums were originally handed down orally and though it is uncertain as to when they were written, it has been suggested that such efforts began in the second or third centuries A.D.[4] and continued through the seventh or eighth century. Targum exegesis not only provides a kind of summary of early Jewish thought but also provides important information for the study of the early Church. Recently, in fact, Targums have been studied for their relevance to the New Testament.[5]

Targums on Pentateuch were among the earliest to be expounded,[6] and it is among these that we find conflicting views of Cain and his possible repentance. Though the interpretations have all been generally classified as Palestinian Targum traditions, they are varied. It has been suggested that the Hebrew text of verse 13 of Genesis 4 may have been a source of conflict in the Targumic interpretations of Cain and his possible repentance. The Hebrew (Masoretic) text in translation reads: "My punishment is greater than I can bear."[7] Apparently there was some confusion or double meaning in the Hebrew phrase *nāśā 'āwôn* which can mean "to bear (i.e., to be burdened with) sin," or, "to forgive (i.e., to take away) sin."[8] Three Targums (as translated) will illustrate the important difference:

1. *Cairo Geniza Fragment.* (The Cairo Geniza was part of the synagogue in Old Cairo; fragments from a Palestinian Targum tradition have been found among the manuscripts representing recensions that not only differ from each other but differ among themselves.)[9] This Targum suggests a view that Cain was repentant and that the Lord will forgive him:

And Cain said before the Lord: Many are my sins, more than to be defended, and they are many before you to be absolved and forgiven.[10]

2. *Pseudo-Jonathan Targum.* (Pseudo-Jonathan is the name used for a complete Targum to the whole of the Pentateuch. It represents a Babylonian version of the Palestinian Targum tradition in a very developed form and is late in its final redaction (post-Muhammad), yet contains material that may go back to pre-Christian times.)[11] This Targum even more strongly suggests a plea for forgiveness by Cain which the Lord might answer affirmatively:

And Cain said before *the Lord:* Severe indeed is my rebellion, more than to be borne, and yet it is possible with you to forgive it.[12]

The idea of sincere repentance (and at least partial forgiveness) is in fact further evidenced in the Pseudo-Jonathan by its Targum on Genesis 4:24:

Now Cain who had sinned and turned in repentance had seven generations extended to him.

There are other Palestinian Targums that also indicate that they construed Cain's words as repentance.[13]

3. *Targum Onkelos.* (This is the Targum that ultimately became the so-called official Targum,[14] but itself was influenced by other Targum traditions and in turn influenced them. It frequently (though not always) tends to remain more of a translation and stays closer to the Hebrew text. Its origin is uncertain, but it may have been brought to Babylonia before the end of the third century A.D. where it received various later redactions.)[15] It is here that the viewpoint that Cain was not repentant is expressed. This Targum emphasizes the iniquity of Cain:

And Cain said before the Lord: Great is my guilt, more than to be forgiven.[16]

This interpretation expressed in Targum Onkelos is in fact the viewpoint that is expressed both by the Septuagint ("My crime is too great for me to be forgiven"),[17] and by the Vulgate ("My iniquity is greater than that I may deserve pardon"). The significance of these contrasting viewpoints toward Cain's repentance on interpretations of Cain's mark will be clarified in later discussion.

There is a hint of repentance reflected in the writings of Flavius Josephus, the Jewish historian who lived about A.D. 37 to 100. In his work known as the *Jewish Antiquities* (ca. A.D. 94) where he traced the history of the Jews in twenty books—from the creation of the world to the beginning of the Jewish war—he expressed views that are best described as those of a fence-sitter. Josephus saw Cain two ways, both evident from his expressions in Book I. He suggests a partially forgiven Cain (because of Cain's sacrificial offering): "God, however, exempted him from the penalty merited by the murder, Cain having offered a sacrifice and therewith supplicated Him not to visit him too severely in His wrath."[18] This is, however, only indirect and vague support for a repentant Cain and could be taken as Josephus's explanation for the delay in God's punishment of Cain. For only a few lines later Josephus strongly suggests an impenitent Cain, stating "His punishment, however, far from being taken as a warning, only served to increase his vice."[19] The views of Josephus are not only important as documents of early Jewish thought but are of additional significance because his works were immensely appreciated by the Fathers and by later Christian exegetes—the latter aided by the translations of all of his work from Greek into Latin ordered by Cassiodorus in the sixth century.[20]

Cain's repentance and its power is also stressed in an early Jewish compilation known as the Midrash Rabbah. But before discussing that particular interpretation some information about the meaning of Midrash is necessary. *Midrash* is a term that applies to interpretation of scripture in general. It is centuries long and of different types.[21] Midrash in its many forms has been a continuous creation from possibly the period of Ezra to the eleventh century.[22] In periods later than that most texts became only anthologies with little or no new material added. The popularity of midrashic interpretations for Jews throughout their history can scarcely be exaggerated. Its continuous appeal to both the learned and the laity has lasted to the present day.[23] Nor was midrashic influence restricted to Jews. Midrashic interpretations often shaped both the methods and the content of Christian and Muslim interpretations of scripture, filling them with fascinating folklore and legends.[24]

The Midrash Rabbah (*rabbah* meaning *great*) was originally given to the commentary on Genesis, but later the title was stretched to cover an entire group of commentaries on the Pentateuch and the five Megilloth (Song of Songs, Ruth, Lamentations, Ecclesiastes, and Esther), though they were composed and compiled at different times. Our concern here is of course with Genesis, known in Hebrew as Bereshith. In its written form it has been classified as belonging to the classical Amoraic Midrashim of the early period (A.D. 400–640),[25] and has been described as mostly a Palestinian work of the fifth century.[26] This is of course the period of the actual assembling and editing, preceded by generations of oral interpretation. Midrash Genesis Rabbah—referred to throughout this study as Genesis Rabbah—is anything but a unified text. It reflects a most varied and complex set of interpretations of different periods and of conflicting views, clearly and strikingly apparent in the interpretations dealing with Cain and his possible repentance.

Opposing views appear in the interpretation of the biblical phrase from Genesis 4:16: "And Cain went out from the presence of the Lord." The Genesis Rabbah poses the question, "Whence did he go out?" Then three answers are stated, each following one another without explanation:

R. Aibu said: It means that he threw the words behind him and went out, like one who would deceive the Almighty.

R. Berekiah said in R. Eleazar's name: He went forth like
one who shows the cloven hoof, like one who deceives his
Creator.[27]

But note the extreme opposite view that is expressed
immediately after those two have been stated:

R. Hanina b. Isaac said: He went forth rejoicing, as you
read, *He goeth forth to meet thee, and when he seeth thee, he will
be glad in his heart* (Ex. iv, 14). Adam met him and asked
him, "How did your case go?" "I repented and am recon-
ciled," replied he. Thereupon Adam began beating his face,
crying, "So great is the power of repentance, and I did not
know!"[28]

Polarized sentiments regarding Cain's repentance are
also reflected in the interpretations of Cain's mark or
sign in the Genesis Rabbah. They will be discussed a
little later.

Ideas of a repentant Cain also occur in the Babylonian Talmud (formed in the course of the fifth century).[29] It appears there as explanation for Cain's final
settlement after his wandering in the land of Nod:
"Rab Judah the son of R. Ḥiyya also said: Exile atones
for the half of men's sins. Earlier [in the Cain narra-
tive] it is written, *And I shall be a fugitive and a wanderer;* but later, *And he dwelt in the land of Nod
[wandering].*[30] In other words, half of Cain's curse—to
be a fugitive—was remitted because of his exile.

Repentance was also attributed to Cain in later
Jewish writings, as for example in the *Pirḳê de Rabbi
Eliezer,* a composite work, whose final redaction took
place probably in the eighth or ninth century.[31] This
text belongs to the group of narrative Midrashim,
popular works that freely retold the biblical story,

adding material not in the biblical text. The *Pirķê de Rabbi Eliezer* has also been described as resembling the Pseudo-Jonathan Targum and as "an important witness to a developed stage of exegesis of which the origins are frequently very early indeed."[32] In the commentary on the Cain and Abel story the view is expressed that Cain had repented:

Cain spake before the Holy One, blessed be He: Sovereign of all the worlds! "My sin is too great to be borne," for it has no atonement [or might be read as a question: "Is there no atonement for it?"].[33] This utterance was reckoned to him as repentance, as it is said, "And Cain said unto the Lord, My sin is too great to be borne."[34]

A repentant Cain is also described in the Zohar, that great fundamental book of Cabbalism that is the primary document of Jewish medieval mysticism. Though purporting to be an ancient Midrash, it is generally thought that the Zohar is a work authored by Moses de Leon about 1280.[35] Earlier material though not quoted by the author was incorporated into it, but it is summarized and put into the Zohar's special style.[36] The Zohar describes Cain during his exile as wandering and unable to find any resting place; only after he repented was he given a place to remain:

And he [Cain] wandered about the world without being able to find any resting-place until, clapping his hands on his head, he repented before his Master.[37]

There is far less evidence in Christian thought of attitudes reflecting the viewpoint that Cain was repentant. There are some to be sure, and two of them will be discussed later in this study—a sixth-century Syriac *Life of Abel* and the great nineteenth-century poem-drama, *Cain*, written by Byron—both literary masterpieces. But whether or not Cain was viewed as repentant, the biblical text has been mostly understood as indicating a Cain under divine protection. Cain's protection is stressed by two items in verse 15: the first part threatens any prospective murderer of Cain with sevenfold vengeance; the second part, the so-called mark of Cain, establishes what may have been intended as an apotropaic device. Interpreters have, for the most part, agreed that for one reason or another the Lord wanted Cain to remain unharmed for a period of time. The reasons given for the delay have varied, however, and disagreement about Cain's status during this period has tended to divide interpreters into two camps: those who postulated a prolonged punishment of Cain during that period, and those who believed that punishment was suspended (because of Cain's repentance) during that time.[38] As the evidence is reviewed it will become increasingly clear that the divided approach to the figure of the arch-sinner, concerning both his repentance and his status while he remained alive, influenced the interpretations of his mark.

2
Early Exegesis

Certain eminent and ancient commentators such as Philo, Josephus, Ambrose, Jerome, Basil the Great, and Augustine of Hippo were among those who chose either to merely repeat the biblical text without comment; or moralizing and philosophizing about Cain, they resisted saying anything concrete about the mark. They were more interested in the "why" than in the "what." They discussed whom Cain feared might try to kill him and why God chose to preserve Cain, but they remained remarkably silent about the nature of the mark. God's purpose interested this category of interpreters more than any particulars regarding the material reality and substance of the mark.

Philo (ca. 20 B.C. to ca. A.D. 50), the Jewish thinker born of a priestly family in Alexandria, produced allegorical interpretations of scripture that combined Greek philosophical and Jewish thought, yet whose basic ideas remained profoundly Jewish. He did in fact comment on Cain's sign, but in an equivocal fashion. Philo seemed unable to make up his mind. In his tract known as "The Worse Attacks the Better," he first confessed ignorance, saying:

and what the sign is, he [God] has not pointed out, although he is in the habit of showing the nature of each object by means of a sign, as in the case of events in Egypt when he changed the rod into a serpent, and the hand of Moses into the form of snow, and the river into blood.[1]

Yet he continues, and as though thinking aloud, Philo decides that the mark of Cain was the absence of Cain's death in scripture:

It would seem then that just this is the sign regarding Cain, that he should not be killed, namely that on no occasion did he meet with death. For nowhere in the Book of the Law has his death been mentioned.[2]

Josephus (the Jewish historian mentioned earlier) offered no suggestion as to what the mark of Cain might have been, saying only that the Lord "set a mark upon him by which he should be recognized and bade him depart."[3] Both Philo and Josephus agreed, however, that the mark must have been necessary to protect Cain from attacks by wild beasts.[4] In addition, Philo suggested that Cain might also have had reason to fear his own parents.[5]

Philo's ideas were echoed later by Ambrose who was influenced by Philo's allegorical method and interpretations. He commented on Cain's fears in his *De Cain et Abel* (composed around A.D. 375):

But from what source did he fear death whose parents were the only living beings on earth? There was the possibility that one who broke the ordinances of the Law of God could have had fears of an attack from wild beasts. . . . A person who showed how the crime of parricide could be committed might well fear a parricidal act on the part of his own parents.[6]

But Ambrose added nothing objectively revealing about the specifics of the mark:

Nunc consideremus qua causa dixerit deus: omnis qui
occiderit Cain septies uindictam exsoluet et qua ratione
signum super eum ponitur, ne occidatur parricida. [7]

[Now let us consider the reason for God's statement,
"Whoever kills Cain shall be punished sevenfold," and
why a token was placed upon him so that no one should
kill him, a parricide.][8]

His Latin, however, indicates that he understood the
mark (whatever it was) to have been placed on the
person of Cain. This is clearly certain, for Ambrose
repeated the phrase *super eum*:

quod autem signum posuit super Cain, ne quis eum occideret, reflectere uoluit errantem et beneficio suo inuitare
ad correctionem;[9]

[As regards the token God placed on Cain with the purpose
of protecting him from death at the hands of another, this
may be said. He wanted the wanderer to have time for
reflection and by such kindness inspire him to change his
ways.][10]

Ambrose furthermore emphasized the mark's protective qualities, thus viewing it as a kind of apotropaic
device placed upon the body of Cain. This puts Ambrose in the camp of those who believed God protected Cain so that he would have time to repent and
change his ways.

One can only wonder and guess what Jerome
thought about the mark of Cain, for thus far at least I
have found nothing in his commentaries which gives
any hints. Jerome commented at length on some of
the verses of Genesis 4 in his letter *Ad Damasum*, yet
he seems to have simply ignored the second part of

verse 15. He seems either to have sidestepp[ed] issue of the mark or, possibly, he just was n[ot in]terested in the mark's characteristics. He concentr[ates] on the *why*—why God should have wanted to sa[ve] Cain's life—suggesting that God did not want to en[d] Cain's life by the expedient method of death, for that would have been too kind.[11] Jerome's view of Cain is remarkably different from Ambrose, for Jerome did not suggest that Cain's death was postponed so that he might repent; on the contrary, Jerome states that God wanted to punish Cain through the seventh punishment, or until the seventh generation.[12] Therefore, according to Jerome, God protects Cain only so that he can be more severely punished, and the protection is achieved by the Lord threatening sevenfold punishments on anyone who might try to release Cain from the torments he must suffer—seven-generations-worth of trials and tribulations.[13] Jerome, unlike Ambrose, said nothing about Cain's mark or sign serving as a protective device. Nor did his contemporary, Augustine of Hippo, contribute finite details to the concept of the mark. Augustine's concern lay in its allegorical implications, and formed part of his typological comparison of Cain and the Jews. Its far-reaching and long-lasting effect makes it worthy of fuller discussion later in this study.

Basil the Great, like Ambrose, Jerome, and Augustine, offered no substantive information about the mark, yet unlike them he viewed God's intention differently. He unequivocally underscored the denigrating aspects of the mark, listing it (though not describing it) as the seventh and worst of seven punishments

re visited upon Cain for his seven sins. The
ments were elaborated in Basil's *Letter to
op Optimus*,[14] probably written in A.D. 377: (1)
cursing of the earth; (2) Cain must till the earth;
) and though Cain till it, the earth will remain fruit-
less; (4) and (5) he is doomed to a continual state of
groaning and trembling; (6) he is to be separated from
God; and (7) a sign is put upon him by the Lord. With
regard to this last Basil said:

This is the seventh punishment: that his punishment was
not even concealed, but that by a conspicuous sign it was
proclaimed to all that this man was the contriver of unholy
deeds. For, to one who reasons rightly, the severest of chastisements is shame.[15]

Basil's notion of the mark as a shameful punishment is a concept that will recur. The groaning and
trembling mentioned by Basil as Cain's fourth and
fifth punishments (God's curse in the Septuagint text
itself) became one of the major interpretations of the
mark of Cain; it will be discussed later. Contrasting
viewpoints are thus already evident in early Christian commentaries. Ultimately, the mark becomes so
overwhelmingly thought of as a humiliating punishment that it loses all its protective aspects. Cain's protection will then seem to derive more from the Lord's
threat of vengeance (as it does in Jerome's exposition), than from any protective elements associated
with the mark.

It is evident that although much was said during the early Christian period about why a mark for
Cain, little interest was shown in precisely what the
mark actually was by well-educated, metaphysically-

oriented thinkers such as Philo, Josephus, Ambrose, Jerome, and Augustine. They were men trained to deal with abstruse sacred mysteries and were accustomed to living with abstract theological concepts. Heightened interest in tangible details concerning the mark of Cain (as well as other parts of scripture) has frequently come from other elements in society—the so-called vulgar, primitive, or popular. Less sophisticated minds, more at home with concrete data than with metaphysical ideas, have frequently dwelt with affection upon homely particulars. The eccentric details of a person or incident have seemed necessary aids to approaching and understanding the sacred world of holy people and pious ideas. Although this has been a somewhat unchanging aspect of the popular or naive mind during any period of history, yet one can note an intensification of interest in the tangible and temporal aspect of sacred things at various times and places. Exegesis as revelation never ceases, but sometimes a significant shift toward exegesis as description, with concrete details underscoring the specific and literal data associated with the holy is especially notable. Writings and documents of various kinds from different strata of societies frequently reflect quite different ideas of a less sophisticated and less traditional nature. In short, the need to deal with the "heavenly" in "earthly" terms is more urgently expressed in some periods and in some places than in others—both in Jewish and Christian circles.

A zesty interest in specificity about the mark of Cain appears, for example, in the Genesis Rabbah that was described earlier with reference to Cain's repentance where the emphasis is distinctly on the nature of

ain's mark rather than on why God decided to provide him with protection. Seven different interpretations are offered in Bereshith XXII, 12:[16]

R. Judah said: He caused the orb of the sun to shine on his
account. Said R. Nehemiah to him: For that wretch He
would cause the orb of the sun to shine! Rather, he caused
leprosy to break out on him; . . . Rab said: He gave him a
dog. Abba Jose said: He made a horn grow out of him. Rab
said: He made him an example to murderers. R. Hanin
said: He made him an example to penitents. R. Levi said in
the name of R. Simeon b. Lakish: He suspended judgment
until the Flood came and swept him away . . .[17]

These varied and contradictory interpretations demonstrate the different attitudes toward Cain discussed
earlier in this study. If his repentance was thought to
have occurred and moreover was believed to be sincere, the nature of the sign that God appointed for
Cain's protection tended to be characterized as a positive boon and benefit. But if the opposite view pre-
vailed and the rabbis saw him as a type of utter per-
verseness whose repentance was feigned, or if they
believed that he in fact never repented, the mark took
on the character of a blight symbolizing total condemnation. But beyond these considerations it is interesting to note that these midrashic interpretations
lend themselves to characterization by genre: (I)
Events (two): The Lord caused the orb of the sun to
shine,[18] and, judgment suspended until the Flood; (II)
Bodyguard (one): gave him a dog; (III) *Cain is himself the
sign*[19] (two): a sign to other murderers, and the opposite, a sign for penitents (because of his repentance);
(IV) *Body markings or changes* (two): leprosy broke out

on him, and a horn grew out of him. These early midrashic interpretations testify to how wide a range of categorical types existed in the minds of men, but in fact it is the genre associated with Cain's person that has constituted the largest proportion of interpretations in both Jewish and Christian thought—whether the mark was construed positively or negatively. Interpretations of the mark associated with Cain's body can be grouped together into roughly three categories, providing both an interesting and convenient way to analyze some of the more prevalent interpretations for Cain's mark. I will deal with each of these three major categories under the following headings: a mark on Cain's body; a movement of Cain's body; and a blemish associated with Cain's body.

3

The Mark Associated with Cain's Body

A MARK ON CAIN'S BODY

As I mentioned earlier, the popular conception of the mark of Cain has tended to see it as a brand-stigma placed on a criminal. Equally prevalent has been the view that the mark was located on Cain's forehead. This misconceived interpretation became so pervasive that it infected the description of the Cain and Abel story in at least two encyclopedia articles. In the *New Schaff-Herzog Encyclopedia of Religious Knowledge* (1908), under *Cain, Kenites*, the author says: "The mark of Cain worn on the forehead, must have denoted adherence to the worship of Yahweh."[1] The author has not only ignored the text of Genesis 4:15 but also has interjected (as though it too were actually part of the biblical text) the modern critical view that the Kenites themselves wore a tribal mark. Even more amazing is the error that appears in the *New Catholic Encyclopedia* (1967), under *Cain and Abel*, where the author states: "After the fratricide, Cain was condemned to the life of a nomad, and God put a sign on his forehead signifying that blood revenge will be exacted if he is killed."[2] Even more recently in an article about the possible influence of Babylonian flood legends on the Bible, published in the *Biblical Archeologist* (December 1977), the author repeats this error about Cain saying, "However, he is not killed. In fact, he becomes one of 'God's protected' and is marked with a special sign on his forehead to indicate that Cain's punishment (if any) is the Lord's and that whoever kills him will be subject to seven-fold retribution."[3] Apparently these authors neglected to reread the biblical text!

The popular misconception (criminal-branded-on-forehead) and the "scholarly" errors in the articles just quoted (Cain-wearing-a-cultic-mark) represent two different traditions; yet each is related to the historically ubiquitous practice of human branding or body marking.[4] Human branding has been used to punish, humiliate, and identify criminals.[5] And it has been used with similar intention to mark other persons deemed objectionable by society at various times, as for example: heretics,[6] vagabonds,[7] brawlers,[8] deserters,[9] and Jews.[10] The practice is at least as ancient as the Greeks[11] and as modern as the Holocaust with the tattooing of numbers on Jews placed in concentration camps.[12] Human branding has also been used until near-modern times for another kind of identification—to establish ownership. The Greeks used the delta, Δ, for *doulos* (slave),[13] the French galley slaves were branded with "TF"—*travaux forcés*—(legal in France until 1832),[14] and American runaway slaves were branded, at least until the American Revolution.[15]

Body marking, however, has also been omnipresent in human history for quite another, more positive purpose—namely, to represent a cult, and thereby achieve the protection of the tribe and its god or gods. Nor are such cultic markings relevant only for ancient peoples and primitive cultures. Christian pilgrims, medieval and modern, have, for example, been tattooed with favorites such as Saint George on horseback, Christ on the Cross, the Virgin Mary holding the infant Jesus, Peter and the crowing cock, and other sacred symbols regarded with reverence because of the magical protection they provided.[16] Marking of the body, whether intended for punishment, for identification, or for cultic protection, has been accomplished in a variety of ways: painting, stamping, sealing, burning, tattooing, and cutting, and has been performed on all parts of the body. Especially common, however, was the face (forehead and cheeks), and the arm (including the hands), and there is the significant rite of circumcision which I will deal with in a Cain-related context later in this study. Thus the idea of a brand (criminal or cultic) so ever present in society may readily have influenced interpretations of Cain's mark.

But aside from the historical ubiquity of the practice of human branding, erroneous conceptions may have been encouraged too by the marks or signs mentioned in both the Old and New Testaments indicating apotropaic devices, or cultic identification, or both. Biblical sources reveal that both the forehead and the arm (or hand) were believed to be eminently appropriate places for special markings. The marking of the foreheads in Ezechiel 9:4 and 6 is especially noteworthy for it demonstrates a distinctly apotropaic use:

And the Lord said to him: Go through the midst of the city, through the midst of Jerusalem: and mark Thau upon the foreheads of the men that sigh, and mourn for all the abominations that are committed in the midst thereof.

Utterly destroy old and young, maidens, children and women: but upon whomsoever you shall see Thau, kill him not, . . .

A cultic and protective principle is also evident in signs on foreheads in Apocalypse 7:3, where the angel says:

Hurt not the earth, nor the sea, nor the trees, till we sign the servants of our God in their foreheads.

And as continued in Apocalypse 9:4, where the locusts and scorpions are commanded to hurt only, "the men who have not the sign of God on their foreheads."

But the opposite principle also functions in the Apocalypse—the concept of an identifying mark or sign that denotes evil. Thus persons devoted to the cult of the evil beast (devil) wear the sign of the beast on their forehead or their hands, and bear negative associations as is stated in Apocalypse 14:9–10:

And the third angel followed them, saying with a loud voice: If any man shall adore the beast and his image, and receive his character [branding or marking] in his forehead, or in his hand;

He also shall drink of the wine of the wrath of God, which is mingled with pure wine in the cup of his wrath, and shall be tormented with fire and brimstome in the sight of the holy angels, and in the sight of the Lamb.

Later (chapter 20, verse 4) we learn that only those lived and reigned with Christ a thousand years who had not adored the beast nor his image, "nor received his character [branding or marking] on their foreheads, or in their hands."

To wear the sign of the right cult was certainly important in the ancient world. This is demonstrated by Aaron himself, the first High Priest of the Old Testament, sanctified and identified with his cult by a plate of gold engraved with a special inscription which he is instructed to wear on his forehead. Directions for designing the plate of the mitre, and for wearing it, are stated in Exodus 28:36–38:

36: Thou shalt make also a plate of the purest gold: wherein thou shalt grave with engraver's work, Holy to the Lord.

37: And thou shalt tie it with a violet fillet, and it shall be upon the mitre.

38: Hanging over the forehead of the high priest. And Aaron shall bear the iniquities of those things which the children of Israel have offered and sanctified. . . . And the plate shall be always on his forehead, that the Lord may be well pleased with them.

Moreover, those worshiping Yahweh of the Old Testament were enjoined to preserve the testimony of the Exodus with the words of the law worn on forehead and hands as expressed in Deuteronomy 6:8, "And thou shalt bind them as a sign on thy hand, and they shall be and shall move between thy eyes," and in Deuteronomy 11:18, "Lay up these my words in your hearts and minds, and hang them for a sign on

your hands, and place them between your eyes."
These verses have had an important and continuing
impact in Jewish tradition in the use of *tefillin* in
prayer. The sign of the tefillin (usually translated,
"phylacteries") is placed on the forehead and on the
left arm, a sacred and ancient custom still practiced by
Orthodox Jews, commonly known as the laying of
the tefillin.[17] The tefillin are two black leather boxes
containing scriptural verses, joined together by black
leather strips on the left hand and the head, and worn
for morning services on all days of the year except
on the sabbath or on certain other holy days. Some
scholars have tentatively suggested that the practice
derived from a form of amulet or charm,[18] but it is
not conclusive. The line between superstition on the
one hand, and pious belief on the other is extremely
fuzzy; whether something is believed to be magic or
devout religion often only reflects the viewpoint of
the interpreter. But we need only be concerned here
with the fact that for one reason or another a continuing significance has been attached to placing signs or
marks on heads (forehead) and hands (or arm).

The brief sketch that I have given of the historical
practice of branding, both for criminal and cultic pur-
poses, and the biblical evidence of the marking of
foreheads (and arms or hands), may help explain why
Cain's mark has frequently been interpreted as some
kind of a mark on his forehead. Just such an interpretation in fact appears in Jewish thought at an early
time. Cain is described as marked on his forehead
with a letter of the Lord's name in the Pseudo-
Jonathan Targum that was mentioned earlier where

Cain's repentance was viewed as sincere.[19] It occurs in the Targum to Genesis 4:15:

And the Lord marked on the face of Cain a letter from the great and glorious name, that any finding him should not kill him when they saw it on him.[20]

According to Jewish tradition the tetragrammaton (YHWH) was a most holy sign conveying divine protection.[21] It was generally thought to be reserved for only the just.[22] It is certainly noteworthy that it is the Pseudo-Jonathan Targum that provided such a positive interpretation of the mark of Cain, for it dramatically focuses on the linking of a positive view toward Cain's repentance with a mark or sign for Cain that is an emblem of honor and protection.

A sacred and divine letter to save Cain. This idea appears also in the *Pirķê de Rabbi Eliezer*, but not on Cain's forehead, and not from the Lord's name, but rather, a letter from the Torah was placed on Cain's arm:

He took one letter from the twenty-two letters and put it on Cain's arm that he should not be killed—[23]

Again this represents a concordance of ideas between a repentant Cain that was noted in this tract earlier in this study, and a mark on Cain with positive connotations. Torah was sacred scripture par excellence and a letter from it denoted divine protection and positive associations. It occurs also in the Zohar (discussed earlier), but the text does not say where on Cain's body the letter was placed:

Therefore the Lord appointed a sign for Cain. This sign was one of the twenty-two letters of the Torah, and God set it upon him to protect him.[24]

The Zohar commentary similarly reflects a positive attitude toward Cain's repentance.[25]

A letter of the Lord's name inscribed on Cain's forehead seems to have had a long life in Jewish thought, for it turns up in the exposition of the famous French eleventh-century Jewish exegete known as Rashi, so called from the initials of his name, Rabbi Solomon ben Isaac:

And the Lord set a sign for Cain. He engraved on his forehead a letter of His [Holy] name.[26]

Rashi, however, did not stress Cain's repentance. Instead he suggested that God merely did not wish to take revenge on Cain at that precise moment, but that he would execute judgment later when Cain will be killed by his descendant, Lamech.[27]

There is early evidence also in at least one Christian source of a mark or sign on Cain's forehead. It occurs in a remarkable composition of about the late fifth or early sixth century known as a Syriac *Life of Abel*, attributed to a certain Symmachus.[28] The actual identity of the author remains unknown and though his name is Greek it seems certain that the original composition was in Syriac.[29] It is a precocious literary treatment of the Cain and Abel biblical story, composed with an emphatic naturalism and a profound concern with the whole range of human feelings that is not met until much later. Even though one knows the biblical story, a reading of Symmachus's *Life of Abel* creates tension, drama, and a sense of pathos for all the characters that is without parallel until Byron's poem-drama, *Cain*, of the nineteenth century. The author of this extraordinary *Life of Abel* achieved a tragic greatness in his original treatment of the theme, reflecting his own keen insight into human character that seems strangely modern. In his development of the story, Symmachus also had much to say about the physical appearance of Cain. In his description is the statement that Cain, returning home after the murder, had a sign on his forehead. At this moment Cain's parents know nothing about the heinous deed. They had already questioned Cain earlier about Abel's disappearance, but Cain had lied to them, saying that he had seen Abel snatched up and had seen him enter Paradise.[30] Adam and Eve, though concerned about Abel's disappearance, and ignorant of Cain's deed, are appalled to see Cain in a horrible condition:

When Cain arrived home, his parents lifted up their eyes and saw him, and they imagined that he was staggering from excess of wine. But when his mother saw his shaking and trembling and the terrible *sign* on his forehead, she laid her hands on her head, and from her mouth there poured forth incessant wails.[31]

What was the terrible sign? Was it terrible in terms of a denigrating brand-stigma, or, was it terrible in the sense of an awe-inspiring letter of the tetragram? The context makes it difficult to decide,[32] for Symmachus writes his story with an unusually sympathetic attitude toward Cain, describing Cain's repentance in great detail. It is in fact through Cain's repentance (which is treated as completely sincere) that Adam and Eve finally discover that Abel has been murdered by Cain:

Cain had neglected to weep at his circumstances, but he (now) began to weep for his brother Abel, for the heart of stone that he had acquired was crushed, and his pity was stirred for his brother; just as he had hated him before killing him, so his love returned after he had killed him. Thus he began to weep for his brother, and to say:

"O Abel my brother, may these eyes of mine consume away—because (*or* which) they saw your tears and had no pity on you; and may these ears of mine grow deaf, because they were stopped at your suppliant cry. O that someone would give you back to me in this humiliation that has come upon me, my brother; would that someone would remove the dust from your eyes, and so you might see what a low estate has befallen your mother's son!"[33]

Not only does Symmachus emphasize Cain's repentance but he creates an Eve who laments the fate of both her sons.[34] The clear-cut repentance of Cain, plus Eve's sorrow over both her sons, suggest a meaning of "terrible sign on Cain's forehead" more akin to the holy and cult-protecting letter of the Lord's name than a stigmatic criminal brand.

Symmachus's *Life of Abel* stands almost alone; not only because of its extraordinary literary merit but because it preserves early evidence in Christian thought of a mark or sign on Cain's forehead. In the ancient and medieval periods of Christian exegetical thought there is little evidence that the idea of a sign or mark on Cain's forehead or elsewhere on his body was frequently offered as an interpretation. Nor does it appear frequently in literature or art. The allusions to Cain's mark in literature when they do occur are often as uninformative as the biblical text itself. In *Beowulf,* for example, the *morþre gemearcod*[35] ("marked with murder") of line 1264 does not tell us much. The Old English *Genesis A* merely paraphrases the biblical verse,[36] as does the late thirteenth-century English poem known as *Cursor Mundi.*[37]

There is evidence of a somewhat more detailed kind that does occur here and there in later periods, and though sparse, it does indicate that the tradition of a mark on Cain's body was well known. The traces that remain suggest that it may have been best preserved by elements of the population outside the mainstream of Christian exegetical thought. It appears, for example, in two medieval dramas—one French, the other English.

A mark on Cain's forehead is mentioned in the mid-fifteenth-century French mystery play written by Arnoul Greban known as the *Mystère de la Passion,*[38] and though details about the nature of the mark are not offered, it is clearly a sign placed on Cain's forehead:

CAYM

Helas, et quel signe en aray je
pour quoy congnoistre le pourront?

DIEU LE PERE

Cestuy signe aras en ton front
pour ta seureté plus accroistre.[39]

[CAIN]

[Alas, and what sign shall I have
So that they will recognize it?]

[GOD THE FATHER]

[This sign will be on your forehead
In order to further increase your security.]

Arnoul Greban was trained as a theologian, and it has been suggested that he consulted theological works for the creation of his *Passion*.[40] There is nothing however that I have thus far found which would indicate that he derived his idea of a sign on Cain's forehead from Christian exegetical writings. Greban was a man of considerable learning and was well acquainted with other materials including earlier Passion plays, legendary stories, and apocryphal writings of various kinds.[41] But wherever and however he found his sign for Cain's forehead, it was popularized by his drama. Greban's play according to Grace Frank was "the most famous of all the great French *Passions*,"[42] for many manuscripts of it have survived and it is known that it was performed not only in Paris, but in Le Mans, Amiens, and Mons. The notion that Cain was marked with a sign on his forehead must have been reinforced among the audiences who have watched and listened to this drama over a long span of time. A copy was requested as early as 1452;[43] it was played in Paris at least three times before 1473;[44] and it has been performed at various times in the twentieth century.[45]

Another example of a mark placed on Cain's body occurs in medieval drama, this time English. It appears in one of the early fifteenth-century York (Corpus Christi cycle) plays where (just as in the French play by Greban) no specifics about the characteristics of the mark itself are described. Moreover, in the York play there is no information as to where on Cain's body the mark was placed. But in sharp contrast to Greban's *Passion* where the mark was presented as a protective device, the York playwright

conceived the mark as a denigrating badge, "prentyd" on Cain by an angel instead of the Lord:

ANGEL.   Nay, Cayme nouȝt soo, haue þou no drede,
   Who þat þe slees shalle ponnysshed be
   Sevene sithis for doyng of þat dede;
   For-thy a token shal þou see,
   It shalle be prentyd so in þe,
   That ilke aman shalle þe knowe full wele
   Caym. Thanne wolle I ffa[r] dir flee for shame.[46]

Cain's protection as described in this York play does
not derive from his mark but only from the threat of
seven punishments on anyone who might kill Cain.
The token printed on Cain is to identify him and his
evil deed so that everyone will know who he is and
what he has done. Stigmatized with his disgraceful
mark Cain himself says that he must flee because of
the shame attached to it. The words convey the mes-
sage of a humiliating brand. The sense of "prentyd"
distinctly suggests branding with a hot iron. It was
probably understood by the audience as the same
kind of imprinted or impressed mark that was cur-
rently placed on heretics, Jews, and criminals, which I
discussed earlier in this study. The Corpus Christi
drama, holding the stage for more than two hundred
years, was as V. A. Kolve put it, "the most truly
popular drama England has ever known."[47] This
alone helps account for the present-day commonplace
image of the mark of Cain as the mark on a criminal.

   The description of the "signe en ton front" in the
French *Passion* and the token "prentyd so in þe," of
the York play, though scanty evidence, are sufficient
to show that by the end of the Middle Ages the notion of a mark on Cain's body had taken hold and was

amply disseminated by the performances themselves. The description of the marking of Cain in the York play in fact anticipates the interpretation so magnificently incorporated by Byron in his nineteenth-century poem-drama *Cain*. Byron's *Cain* (published in 1821) shocked most of his contemporaries who saw it as a blasphemous exposition. The whole fascinating history of critical reaction to Byron's poem has been published by Truman Steffan.[48] The criticism of Byron's dramatic poem, both in the nineteenth and twentieth centuries, reveals more perhaps about the critics than the work criticized, but that has been true of critical perspectives from time immemorial.

Byron like the York dramatist used an angel as a "stand-in" for God, and like that medieval English playwright, Byron portrayed the mark as a brand, though definitely a brand on Cain's forehead:

ANGEL.   The fratricide might well engender parricides.
　But it shall not be so. The lord thy God
　And mine commandeth me to set his seal
　On Cain so that he may go forth in safety.
　Who slayeth Cain, a sev'nfold vengeance shall
　Be taken on his head. Come hither.
CAIN.   What
　Wouldst thou with me?
ANGEL.   To mark upon thy brow
　Exemption from such deeds as thou hast done.
CAIN.   No, let me die!
ANGEL.   It must not be.
　　　(The ANGEL *sets the mark on* CAIN'S *brow.)*
CAIN.   It burns
　My brow, but naught to that which is within it.
　Is there more? Let me meet it as I may.

In this context the mark carries exemption; Cain is protected, but as was so often the case with the mark, it was also simultaneously Cain's humiliating punishment. Two earlier poems by Byron referred to a mark on a criminal's brow.[49] Byron's concept of the mark of Cain epitomizes our understanding today of the mark as a stigmatic mark on the forehead, yet it is also the descendant of what may have been the ordinary man's understanding of it in the Middle Ages and Renaissance.

The mark of Cain or the marking of Cain's body is a theme that was not frequently represented in the visual arts, unlike the scene of the cursing of Cain by the Lord. There are two examples of the actual marking of Cain by the Lord which I have thus far located—one in England, the other in Italy, both in the fourteenth century. (Other examples of a mark on Cain that belong best to the category of the mark as a blemish will be discussed later.) The English Bohun Psalter (Oxford Bodleian MS. Auct. D.4.4.)[50] of about 1370, contains an unusually full representation of the Cain and Abel story in five scenes all depicted on folio 40 (fig. 1). In the upper left Cain is eating fruit, while Eve suckles Abel; to the right, the two brothers bring their respective sacrifices to the Lord; in the next lower scene at the left, Cain kills Abel with the famous jawbone of an ass,[51] and immediately to the right, Cain, standing but still holding the jawbone murder weapon, is in some uncertain way touched by the Lord on his right cheek, that is, the Lord is depicted in the process of marking him. (See the detail, fig. 2). The Lord seems to be holding something in his hand, but what it is is difficult to identify. Could it be a branding iron? Cheeks were also frequently designated places for criminal branding.[52] (The fifth scene, third lowest on the left, depicts the legendary death of Cain—killed by his descendant Lamech—which will be discussed more fully later.)

Another full cycle of Cain and Abel scenes was part of the fresco decoration of the Camposanto at Pisa (A.D. 1390),[53] unfortunately damaged in a fire in 1944 (fig. 3). The photograph, however, clearly shows: (1) Cain bringing his sheaf of wheat and Abel his lamb—the accepted lamb consumed by fire issuing from the half figure of God; (2) at the right, Cain killing Abel with a club; (3) above and slightly to the left, God cursing Cain; and (4) to the right of the cursing, Cain is marked by God (see the detail, fig. 4). (The remaining two scenes again represent the Lamech legend that will be discussed later.) The marking scene is difficult to precisely interpret. It consists of beamlike rays that project both from heaven and from the Lord; they extend and touch Cain's forehead and his cheek and chin, but at the same time they look like phylacteries containing inscriptions. I have not been able to decipher them; however, they may contain biblical verses appropriate to the scenes. At the present time these two examples in the visual arts are the only ones I have located of an actual marking of Cain by God, or a mark on Cain (as distinguished from physical blemishes or growths). There may be others I have overlooked, yet it is conclusively certain that this biblical event was rarely depicted.

It is Cain's counterpart—a close "cousin" known as the Wandering Jew[54]—who was ultimately vividly depicted with a stunning mark on his forehead. The legend of the Wandering Jew, one of many extrascriptural legends circulating in the early period of Christianity, gradually took shape, and though it had endless variations, it was a story that went generally like this: When Christ was carrying his Cross, he paused to rest on a certain man's doorstep but the man drove Christ away, shouting at Christ: "Walk faster!" Christ replied, "I go, but you will walk until I come again!" The Wandering Jew (of different names and places, but frequently known as Ahasuerus) and Cain, have shared many attributes. Both were outcasts from God and from the society of men; both were eternal wanderers; and both were believed to have longed for death. Cain may in fact have furnished inspiration for the genesis of the legend of the Wandering Jew. Misconceived ideas about Cain's mark were not surprisingly transferred to the Wandering Jew, but they were late arrivals to that legend.[55] When a special kind of mark, therefore, appeared in literature and art on the forehead of the Wandering Jew, it is certainly the result of the conflation of ideas about the two figures. Since it probably represented commonly held notions about Cain's mark, it is of interest to us here. This transmutation of Cain's mark appears first in a subplot of Matthew Gregory Lewis's *The Monk* (London, 1796).[56] In this story a certain Raymond is saved from a horrible vampire by the Wandering Jew who is described as a man of majestic personality, with an awe-inspiring glance. The feature of his costume, which is otherwise plain, is a band of black velvet which encircles his forehead. This man assures Raymond that he can drive away the vampire, saying:

The hungry tiger shudders at my approach, and the alligator flies from a monster more horrible than itself. God has set his seal upon me, and all his creatures respect this fatal mark. . . .

He put his hand to the velvet which was bound round his forehead. There was in his eyes an expression of fury, despair, and malevolence that struck horror to my very soul. . . .[57]

Then the Wandering Jew finally purges the room of the vampire by unveiling his mark:

He spoke in a commanding tone, and drew the sable band from his forehead. In spite of his injunctions to the contrary, curiosity would not suffer me to keep my eyes off his face. I raised them, and beheld a burning cross impressed upon his brow.[58]

The Wandering Jew was so depicted in art. He appeared in a popular picturization with a red cross vividly depicted on his forehead. It is especially striking in a color woodcut done by Gustave Doré in 1852 reproduced here in black and white (figs. 5, 6). It is still uncertain whether this popularization was due to the Lewis novel or to a well-established folkloristic tradition.[59] Though this mark on the Wandering Jew appears earliest in the Lewis novel, it has been suggested that it is part of an older tradition and analogous to the mark of Cain.[60] In fact it is cited as one of the interpretations of Cain's mark in Pierre Bayle's famous *Dictionnaire historique et critique* (1695–1697),[61] thus pushing the idea of a cross on Cain's forehead as his mark back at least to the seventeenth century. The actual portrayal in art of the Wandering Jew with the red cross may, however, owe most to the Lewis novel, for it was extremely popular and read by thousands.[62] Yet all these related documents—literary and visual—owe their lives to the delicate but tenacious ties between fact and fiction and between the Wandering Jew and Cain.

A MOVEMENT OF CAIN'S BODY

While Byron's burning brand on Cain's forehead or the cross on the Wandering Jew may mirror popular ideas about the mark of Cain, yet these do not reflect the most favored interpretation throughout the history of Christian thought. A more consistently approved exposition of Cain's mark falls into the second category of interpretation that I mentioned earlier—a movement of Cain's body. The verses of the Septuagint—that Cain must tremble and mourn[63]—were ultimately interpreted as his mark. What seems to have happened is that the trembling and mourning, originally understood as Cain's curse and one or two of the major punishments visited upon him, were gradually transformed into the mark itself. Early Christian exegetes lingered lovingly on their elucidations of the trembling and groaning prescribed for Cain, yet they did not suggest that these punishments also constituted the mark or sign of Cain. Ambrose said, for example:

How can Cain, when he is not absolved by the earth, be absolved by the righteous decisions made there above? Hence he is commanded to be "a fugitive on the earth, groaning and trembling."[64]

And Basil, it will be recalled, mentioned the groaning and trembling as the fourth and fifth punishments of Cain, and described them vividly:

> He [the Lord] has added two to the other three—continual groaning, and trembling of the body, since his limbs had not the support that comes from strength. For since he had used the power of his body wickedly, his vigour was taken away, so that he tottered and shook, being unable easily either to bring bread to the mouth or to fetch water to it, his wicked hand not being permitted after the unholy deed even to administer to the private and necessary needs of the body.[65]

Basil, however, did not suggest that they were Cain's mark, for he added that the seventh punishment, an undesignated shameful sign, was added.[66] Augustine also tied trembling and groaning to Cain's punishment, but primarily in his allegorical comparison of Cain with the Jews.[67]

It is Jerome who seems to have added a new element. He alluded to the trembling and moaning as punishment in his letter *Ad Damasum*, but emphasized that they in fact actually divulged Cain's crime:

> I am cast out, he [Cain] says, from your sight, and because of my awareness of the crime, I cannot bear the light itself; I'll sneak away to hide, but it will be that anyone who finds me will kill me, since from the trembling of the body and

from the agitation of my maddened mind everyone will understand that this one [Cain] deserves to be killed.[68]

Jerome does not suggest that the trembling and the agitation of Cain's maddened mind in any way represent the mark of Cain. Jerome's expression, "maddened mind" [*furiatae mentis*] was probably his notion of a concrete manifestation of the moaning or groaning. As I mentioned earlier, Jerome seems not to have discussed Cain's mark in any of his writings, but rather appears to have been content to let Cain's protection depend on the Lord's threat of vengeance on anyone foolish enough to end Cain's suffering by killing him before seven generations had passed.

Procopius described the trembling and moaning as manifestations of mental states: moaning resulting from Cain's sadness; trembling from Cain's fear. He saw them as punishments meant to lead Cain to repentance and salvation. Procopius did not, however, indicate that these chastisements were in any way also intended to serve as the sign or mark of Cain. On the contrary, he stated that the mark was something additional: "A sign was added so that he should not fall by anyone's hand."[69] In his subsequent comment he even hints that the added sign was scarcely necessary because Cain's sin made him infamous enough:

Whoever saw him moaning and trembling, even if he didn't know of the evil deed, and even if he didn't know why the mark had been put on him, nevertheless, by questioning, could hear Cain himself confess his crime and blame himself.[70]

But what was the exact nature of this trembling and groaning? Basil, we saw, did provide details of a Cain shaking and tottering so much that he could scarcely eat or drink. An early Syrian commentary on Pentateuch had this to say: "The fear or trembling restricted his activities, and groaning impeded his speech—the first for the murder of his brother, the second for the insolence of his speech."[71]

Another extraordinarily vivid description occurs in the Syriac *Life of Abel,* though it is never referred to as Cain's mark. Recall that in this case the trembling and the "terrible sign" on Cain's forehead have been combined.[72] They are both visible, but are not recognized as Cain's special sign by Adam and Eve, who see them, comment on them, but are ignorant of their genesis:

What will become of me? My youngest son is no longer, while the one who is left is staggering while still a youth, and before his youth is up his limbs are seized by shaking and trembling!

Adam too wept in grief. . . . And after they [Adam and Eve] had wept, and made each other weep, they sat down to learn about Abel from Cain.[73]

Only after Cain himself begins to weep and repent[74] do Adam and Eve learn the horrible truth; yet Eve continues to mourn both Abel and Cain. The concrete nature of this curse-punishment—though Cain has convincingly repented—is bitingly demonstrated by the words of Eve who cannot decide whom to mourn more—Abel or Cain:

Two sorrows have come upon wretched (me) in a single
day, two blows have befallen me in a single hour. (If) I
turn my eyes to the ground, the corpse of the slain man
gives me pain, and if I raise my eyes then I see this man
shaking and trembling. . . . I do not know which of them
I should lament, I know not which of the two I should
weep for.[75]

Though the author of the *Life of Abel* dealt at length
with the physical state of Cain, he saw the "shaking
and trembling" only as part of God's curse. In his
story they neither divulge Cain's crime nor function
as a protective device. In fact the Syriac author totally
ignores both parts of Genesis 4:15; neither the mark
of Cain nor the Lord's threatened vengeance were
made part of his literary masterpiece. The description
of Cain's physical disabilities, however, precociously
anticipates what will appear in later Christian exegesis.

Although early exegetes did not equate the curse or
the punishments with the mark of Cain, the comments by Basil are significant evidence that the mark
of Cain could be conceived of as a curse or unpleasant
punishment. This rendering became increasingly
common with the passage of time so that no matter
how the mark of Cain was conceived (protective or
not protective), it was also construed as part of his
punishment. Ignominious curse it might be, yet it
identified Cain as someone who must not be touched;
degraded and dishonored, but strictly off limits and
taboo. The rationale, making Cain's curse-punishment his mark, appears early, as for example in the
Ethiopian Adambook, a pseudepigraphical Chris-

tian composition known as the *Conflict of Adam and Eve*, dated fifth or sixth century:[76]

Then the Creator said to him, "Be trembling and quaking." Then Cain trembled and became terrified; and through this sign did God make him an example [or, notorious] before all the creation, as the murderer of his brother.[77]

Also did God bring trembling and terror upon him, that he might see the peace in which he was at first, and see also the trembling and terror he endured at the last; so that he might humble himself before God, and repent of his sin . . .[78]

The description continues and echoes the Syriac *Life*:

But as to Cain, ever since he had killed his brother, he could find no rest in any place; but went back to Adam and Eve, trembling, terrified, and defiled with blood.[79]

As in the *Life of Abel*, Cain's parents are ignorant of the murder committed by Cain:

When they [Adam and Eve] saw him they grieved and wept, not knowing whence came his trembling and terror, and the blood with which he was bespattered.[80]

Cain's deed is made public when he confesses to the sister whom by legend he was born with:

But when she saw him, she was affrighted, and said unto him, "O, my brother, wherefore art thou come thus trembling?" And he said to her, "I have killed my brother Abel in a certain place."[81]

The significant difference then between the Syriac *Life* and the *Conflict of Adam and Eve* is that the trembling in the latter is actually mentioned as Cain's sign, while such attribution is lacking in the Syriac *Life*.

It is difficult to say who was the first to suggest that trembling and moaning were the sign of Cain. Perhaps Jerome's suggestion—that Cain's trembling and agitated mind divulged his crime—was misinterpreted (or misunderstood) so that Jerome's idea that trembling and moaning divulged Cain's crime was taken to mean that they indeed were his mark or sign. Bede (the English biblical scholar and "father of English history" who lived from about 673–735), though possibly not the earliest to pinpoint trembling as Cain's mark, seems to be the first to succinctly and unequivocally state that the mark of Cain was the equivalent of his curse-punishment of moaning and trembling. Bede, moreover, added to it the parallel expressions of the Vulgate (*vagus et profugus*):

This sign—that is—that he should always live trembling and moaning, and wandering and exiled—would warn anyone that Cain was not to be killed. For he who would kill Cain would either liberate Cain from his misery or would subject himself to sevenfold punishment by doing this.[82]

It seems clear then that Bede, or possibly some earlier source, not only combined the ancient Septuagint version (trembling and moaning) with the Vulgate (wandering and exiled) but did so by interpolating a transition into Jerome's commentary, thereby transforming it. By this I mean that instead of the movement of Cain's body (trembling, moaning, wandering, and exiled) only revealing his crime, it had also become a taboo sign; his humiliating human condition protects his life.

Commentators such as Alcuin (the eighth-century English scholar-exegete),[83] and his student Rabanus Maurus[84] (one of the great theologians of his age) repeated Bede's interpretation of the mark of Cain. They added, however, as did Angelomus of Luxeuil (mid-ninth century),[85] an interesting comment demonstrating their scholarly (or religious) anxiety about the curious contradiction of Cain as wanderer and Cain as city builder. They suggested that it was perhaps because Cain did not dare remain quiet [cursed to wander] anywhere in the world, that he built the first city—that is, in order to be safe.[86] It is interesting to see the scholarly sophistication of Remigius of Auxerre (ca. 841–908), the medieval philosopher who followed this interpretation, but wanted to let his readers know that he knew a difference existed between the trembling and moaning derived from the Septuagint and the language of the Vulgate. He in fact changed the order of things, using the Vulgate language first, followed by the Septuagint:

This sign indeed was that he was wandering and exiled on earth, or, as in the Septuagint, groaning and trembling.[87]

Gradually interpretations of Cain's trembling evolve so that later commentaries combine the kind of concrete details of Cain's physical disabilities that appeared in Symmachus's *Life of Abel* with the straightforward statements of Bede, Alcuin, Rabanus Maurus, Angelomus of Luxeuil, and Remigius of Auxerre. Later exegesis reflects an appetite for, and interest in, intimate details and homely particulars. There seems to be a more urgent need to bring the heavenly mysteries down to earth, especially notable from the twelfth century on. In the commentary of Bruno of Asti (who lived ca. 1049–1123), for example, neither the language of the Septuagint nor the Vulgate was used, but rather just *membrorum tremor*:

This sign is said to have been a trembling of the limbs because as if insane and like a melancholic person, he called men's attention to his wretched state. For who would want to kill someone who appeared to suffer things worse than death.[88]

And in the twelfth-century commentary of Hugh of St. Victor, the Victorine theologian, a similar taste for specifics is expressed by Hugh's desire to analyze more precisely what constituted Cain's trembling:

The sign on Cain, it is a trembling of the limbs, like a raving madman, it is of a raging (furious) person, spastic, that is, shaking violently and unable to stand, whence he appeared worthy of pity, that is, because he had been struck by the anger of God and excommunicated.[89]

The down-to-earth comments of Bruno of Asti and Hugh of St. Victor echo the descriptions and language of the early Syriac *Life of Abel*. The difference of course is that the descriptions in the Syriac *Life* were conceived of only as Cain's punishments and not as his mark. Recall that in the *Life of Abel*, Cain was described as "staggering from excess of wine," and mourned over by Eve who said, "while the one who is left [Cain] is staggering while still a youth, and before his youth is up his limbs are seized by shaking and trembling!" Though neither Bruno of Asti nor Hugh of St. Victor suggested drunkenness or the unsteadiness of old age, as descriptive of Cain's trembling, they did suggest distinct physical disabilities— the wild shaking of the insane, the trembling of melancholy, and the uncontrolled movements of a spastic.

A similar interest in particulars appears in the exegesis of Peter Comestor (d. 1179) who, however, shifts the emphasis from Cain's limbs in general to Cain's head, in his famous *Historia Scholastica* which became the standard work on biblical history, serving as a setbook in the schools and as a classic for both clergy and laity.[90] His version was stated thus:

And God put a sign on Cain, a trembling of the head, because he had killed his brother, who was head of the Church, so that he would thus be known as punished and excommunicated by the Lord, and not worthy of mercy, and so that he would not be killed.[91]

Comestor's version, however, makes it evident that both protection and punishment have been achieved in the mark of Cain, for though he believes the punishment fits the crime, and though Cain has been excommunicated by the Lord, the humiliating sign serves as curse, identifying stigma, and safeguard. His notion of a shaking head has the concrete characteristics of another kind of physical disability, what is popularly known as Parkinson's disease.

The tremendous spread and influence of Peter Comestor's *Historia Scholastica* inevitably meant that his rendering of Cain's mark as the movement of Cain's head worked its way into other places. It appears, for example, in the *Aurora*, the popular versified Bible (and Bible commentary) written by Peter Riga between 1170 and 1209:

Therefore, he gives Cain a sign, so that he might not be killed quickly, / And that was a movement and a trembling of the head.[92]

The *Aurora*, one of the most frequently copied books of the Middle Ages, has been described as "a popularization which succeeded—perhaps beyond the wildest hopes of its author."[93] Thus for those who could read Latin (laity as well as clergy), it supplied popular scriptural lore and theology, and along with it helped to spread the idea that Cain's mark was a shaking and trembling of his head.

Peter Comestor's interpretation of Cain's mark as a trembling of the head even reached the eyes of Innocent III, for it appeared in Innocent's famous letter of 1208 addressed to the Count of Nevers:

The Lord made Cain a wanderer and a fugitive over the earth, but set a mark upon him making his head to shake, lest any finding him should slay him.[94]

It surfaced much later too, as for example in a Middle English *Life of Adam and Eve* of about A.D. 1370 to 1380:

"Nay," seide vr lord, "I schal sette a token vp þe, þat alle þat sle Caym, seuenfold schal his synne be more." And þo sette Crist a marke vp on him: þat he waggede alwey forþ wiþ his heued.[95]

That the mark of Cain was a trembling of Cain's limbs (in general and not necessarily only his head) must have had some early popular support, for we learn of it through its condemnation by Rupert of Deutz (ca. 1075–1129), the theologian who attempts to trounce all who accept such an interpretation. In his comments on the Genesis text Rupert emphatically denies that the trembling of the limbs was the mark of Cain.[96] Rupert's denial is of further interest because in it Rupert demonstrates a sophisticated interpretation of the grammar in Genesis 4:15 whereby Cain is the sign, that is, the second possibility discussed at the very beginning of this study: *Posuitque Cain* [in] *signum*, meaning, "made Cain [as] a sign." Rupert, aware of the grammatical possibilities of the biblical passage, says that Cain became the sign of the Lord, thereby representing the Lord's proclamation; and therefore Cain as the sign was the symbol of the ruler which must not be violated. Rupert continued, saying that no one should dare touch Cain for vengeance, for no one should take away the sign of a king or emperor, and wisely so because blood feuds would otherwise be perpetuated.[97]

Rupert attributed the trembling of the limbs and another interpretation—that Cain was marked with a horn[98]—to what he called "Jewish fables."[99] The attribution of the trembling of the limbs interpretation to Jewish thought seems somewhat extraordinary since there is little evidence in Jewish sources of interpretations that the mark was a trembling of Cain's limbs. There is, however, a first-century A.D. commentary by a writer known as the Pseudo-Philo which might be so understood. It appears in his work known as the *Biblical Antiquities of Philo*, a continuous history of Israel from Adam to the death of Saul, containing extensive additions of a legendary character with no scriptural basis and with many scriptural omissions:[100]

Now Cain lived in the earth trembling, as God decreed for him after he killed Abel his brother.[101]

This verse in the Pseudo-Philo text contains no further information, so it is difficult to assess.

Beyond the Pseudo-Philo, I have thus far been able to locate only a vague, but possibly allusively connected comment by Rashi (the eleventh-century French rabbi-exegete discussed earlier). Commenting on Cain's exiled state, Rashi says that, "Wherever he [Cain] went the earth trembled under him. . . ."[102] But Rashi's commentary might more probably reflect the general confusion about the land of Nod. The land of Nod was either thought of as a concrete place, that is, Nod was a place-name, or, it was named because of Cain's wandering. Possibly wandering was equated with trembling, and that might also be the more correct interpretation of the Pseudo-Philo commentary. Nod (or Naid) meant place of wandering, and no exact location was known or, possibly, intended. Interpretations varied,[103] and more sober exegetes sought a symbolic rather than a literal reading for Nod, Jerome among them.[104]

I have already noted the appearance of a mark on Cain's forehead in the French *Passion*, and some kind of a mark "printed" on Cain in the English York play. The tradition of "trembling" as Cain's mark was strong enough to leave an imprint of its own in drama. It appears in late medieval France (early sixteenth century) in the very long play known as *Le mistère du viel Testament*, a disparate compilation of different dates and authors.[105] This drama (or separate parts of it) were frequently performed and achieved great popular success, so much so that a special performance by the Confrérie de la Passion was given in Paris in 1542 for the Duke of Vendôme who having heard much about the *Vieux Testament*, but not having attended a performance, requested that it be performed (at least part of it) for him after dinner.[106] The theme of Cain's trembling occurs again and again in the play. Since this drama represents the only extensive treatment of the trembling theme in literature, those parts merit full quotation:[107]

Lines 2859–2866. Here Cain is actually cursed and marked with this sign:

DIEU

. . .

Pourtant, comme tel malfaicteur	[Nevertheless, as such an evildoer,
Par my la terre vaqueras	You will wander through the world
Et signe sur toy porteras,	And you will carry impressed upon you
De ton grant peché caractére	The sign of your great sin
Pour que tu as tué ton frére	Because you have killed your brother
Toute ta vie trembleras:	You will tremble for your entire life

| Par ce signe congneu seras, | By this sign you will be known, |
| Affin que aucun ne te mefface. | So that no one will harm you.] |

Line 2915. Here Cain's sisters see Cain trembling:

CALMANA

| Comment, Cayn? Il vient tremblant. | [What's this, Cain? He comes trembling.] |

Lines 2980 ff. Delbora says that Cain trembles because he killed Abel:

DELBORA

Cayn l'a de sa propre main	[Cain has killed him with his own hand
Tué, ainsi qu'il nous a dit,	As he has told us.
Et pour ce cas l'a Dieu mauldit;	And for that God has cursed him.
Tout son corps tremble pour ce point	His entire body trembles for that reason,
Et si dit qu'il n'espére point	And thus he says that he has no hope at all
Grace avoir, mais estre damné.	For grace, but to be damned.]

The most elaborate treatment occurs when Cain's son, Enoch, and Enoch's son, Irard, describe the trembling, as in lines 3154–3172:

ENOCH

Mon pére est en perplexité	[My father is in perplexity
Son corps est tout debilité	His body is totally debilitated,
Tremblant; dont luy peult il venir?	Trembling; how then can he move?]

IRARD

Je n'en sçay pas la verité,

Ne discerner la quantité

Du gref mal qui le peult tenir.

[I don't know the truth of it,

Nor can I discern the quantity

Of grave trouble which grips him.]

ENOCH

Ses membres ne peult retenir
De trembler, ne les soustenir;
Tousjours tremble incessamment.

[He cannot stop his limbs

From trembling, nor can he hold them up;
Always he trembles incessantly.]

IRARD

L'auroit bien Dieu voulu pugnir

Et le faire ainsi devenir

Pour la mort d'Abel seulement?

[Would God have wanted to punish him so thoroughly

And make him become thus [as he is]

Just because of the death of Abel?]

ENOCH

Ce seroit cruel jugement,

Mais je cuide certainement
Que c'est debilitacion

Des membres que ce tremblement,
Et non pas pour pugnissement
De divine ordinance.

[That would have been cruel judgment,

But I think certainly
That this trembling is debilitation
Of his limbs

And not the result of punishment
By divine ordinance.]

Cain must, in fact, have trembled on stage, for immediately following God's curse-marking of Cain (following line 2866), the stage instructions state, "Icy tremble [Here, he (Cain) trembles]." There may have been a lot of shaking: Cain trembling on stage each time he appeared; the audience trembling with excitement, with consternation—or who knows—maybe shaking with laughter?

Later Christian exegetes acknowledged that trembling and moaning may have been Cain's sign, but quite often with the qualification of "some say that." For example, the fifteenth-century commentator, Dionysius the Carthusian (Denys van Leeuwen), ca. 1402–1471, whose writings became especially popular in the century after his death, stated:

Which sign or scar was as some say a severe trembling of the head. Others say that it was a horrible trembling of all of his limbs, and with this a certain impression on his face. According to Strabo there was in Cain a trembling of the body and an agitation of his disturbed mind.[108]

The Flemish biblical exegete Cornelius à Lapide (of the early seventeenth century) first recited several interpretations that he believed to have come from the rabbis, but then added:

But the more common opinion is that this sign was a trembling of the body and a disturbance of mind and appearance (face) so that body and appearance spoke Cain's sin. For that this trembling was in Cain is clear from the Septuagint.[109]

And later in the seventeenth century, a whole listing of possible interpretations was offered by Pierre

Bayle in his *Dictionnaire historique et critique* (mentioned earlier with reference to the idea of a cross on Cain's forehead), and among them he describes the trembling as:

Others say he [Cain] became subject to such a trembling, that he could hardly lift his Food to his Mouth. The Septuagint favour this Sentiment . . .[110]

The trembling of Cain's body remained an acceptable Catholic interpretation of the mark of Cain as late as the 1911 Murphy edition of the Douay translation of the Vulgate, where we can still read the annotation provided by Bishop Challoner in 1750:

The more common opinion of the interpreters of holy writ supposes this mark to have been a trembling of the body; or a horror and consternation in his countenance.

A BLEMISH ASSOCIATED WITH CAIN'S BODY

The third category of interpretations associated with Cain's body involves physical blemishes of one kind and another. The suggestion in the Genesis Rabbah that Cain was blighted with leprosy is of this genre; however, this interpretation did not achieve much currency.[111]

Another interpretation, also rare, was that beardlessness was a mark of Cain. It occurs in the twelfth-century Irish *Lebor Gabála Érenn* (The Book of the Taking of Ireland), henceforth referred to as simply *Lebor Gabála*. In this text it has been combined with other elements also listed as part of Cain's mark.[112] This text has been described as a "product of Gaelic learning of the eleventh and twelfth centuries."[113] It includes a huge collection of poems and prose allegedly recounting the history of Ireland from the Creation until the final "taking" of Ireland by a sixth group of invaders, the sons of Míl, descendants of Goedel Glas and supposed ancestors of the warrior ruling class.[114] It is full of fiction and euhemerized myths, and though possibly useless for the study of the history of Ireland, it is a goldmine for those interested in Irish sentiment, myths, and uncanonical biblical material. The recent editor of the *Lebor Gabála* has convincingly argued that the work as a whole is a conflation of two separate books: the first a development of a parallel between the history of the Goedels and the history of Israel; and the second a development of "origins" from euhemerized myths.[115]

Though the interpretation of beardlessness in the *Lebor Gabála* seems to be uniquely Irish, it is interesting to note that in the twelfth-century English Winchester Psalter Judas is depicted distinctively beardless in what appears as an intentional contrast to Christ and the other apostles. It is especially striking in the portrayal of *The Last Supper* (folio 20), but is also evident in the *Betrayal* (folio 21).[116] Beards have been thought to be good or bad, varying with time and place. Thus, beardlessness on an adult man was a demeaning thing in some cultures. And in fact in the Irish context of the *Lebor Gabála* Seth was the man credited with the first beard. He is described in one of its verses as "the man without deficiency upon whom the first beard grew."[117] As the editor explained, Adam was presumably created with his beard, Abel died a beardless youth, and Cain was punished by being beardless; therefore, Seth was the first to have a beard.

Though beardlessness as a blemish for Cain was an uncommon interpretation of the mark, yet it emphasizes the human tendency to describe the mark as a physical fault, or as some aspect of human physiognomy thought ugly and base in a particular culture. Occasionally the idea of deformity or disfigurement was exaggerated to accentuate the beastlike nature of Cain. Cain was born entirely human. Not a demon, demihuman, or monster. But his rapid descent into evil, and his lack of natural feeling so grotesquely displayed in the brother-murder, provoked interpretations that emphasized the bestial quality of his character. Motifs or themes blurring the edges between Cain seen as a beastlike man, and Cain seen as a manlike beast, appeared among the many legends enlarging the biblical story. A partial metamorphosis of Cain, that is, from depraved man into a half human, almost half animal creature is hinted at in one of those early Jewish midrashic interpretations of Cain that I quoted earlier in the Genesis Rabbah—that Cain was marked with a horn. This midrashic interpretation of a horn as the mark of Cain so puzzled Louis Ginzberg that he added a parenthetical question to his citation asking: "Was it meant as a degradation of his human form?"[118] Certainly that is what it seemed to be.

Interpretations of the mark of Cain, as we have seen, frequently turned on whether it was considered a sign of protection or a sign of punishment, on whether Cain was believed to be pardoned or condemned. While the mark of Cain, both in Jewish and Christian thought, came to be overwhelmingly understood as a badge of punishment, some of the earliest interpretations stressed its security features. Cain, exiled, yes, but with a safe conduct pass. The horn may have served in precisely that way when it was originally introduced; that is, possibly in ancient oral exegesis the horn as Cain's sign was introduced as a protective emblem. The exposition in the Genesis Rabbah does not inform us as to whether it was meant as protection or punishment. If it did enter as a protective emblem this would have been in keeping with the meaning of horns at that time. Horns, after all, were honorable in the ancient world. They symbolized kingship, deity, and the abstract qualities of strength, power, and glory, and as such they served as powerful apotropaic devices.[119] Their continued amuletic use in present-day Italy testifies to the tenacious quality of that ancient meaning.

Horns gradually lost most of their more positive connotations and became increasingly associated with the animallike natures of devils and monster-beast types.[120] Along with this change, it was reasonable that the horn of Cain—already present in the ancient lore—was reinterpreted. Its protective connotations disappeared; they were replaced by those implying a degrading and deforming punishment. The horn sprouting from Cain's head became a concrete manifestation of his bestial nature. This is the meaning that was unequivocally intended when the horn as the mark of Cain was welded to the Lamech legend. The horn as Cain's sign rarely appeared alone; it was usually linked with the ancient Lamech legend about the death of Cain.

Like the mark of Cain, biblical silence regarding the death of Cain was quickly remedied by legendary accounts. One legend tells of Cain dying in the Flood;[121] another attributes his death to his own house falling on him.[122] But the belief that he was ultimately killed by his own descendant, Lamech, was the story that became by far the most widespread, both in Jewish and Christian thought. This story evolved as an ingenious invention from the rather unintelligible and ambiguous song of Lamech in Genesis 4, where Lamech says in verses 23 and 24:

> And Lamech said to his wives Ada and Sella: Hear my voice, ye wives of Lamech, hearken to my speech: for I have slain a man to the wounding of myself, and a stripling to my own bruising.
>
> Sevenfold vengeance shall be taken for Cain: but for Lamech seventy times sevenfold.

Out of these verses grew the notion that Lamech was alluding to Cain as the man he had slain and to a second person he murdered, a youth. A legend with numerous variations evolved; in general its outlines went something like this: Lamech, a hunter, having become blind in his old age, was led about by a youth, sometimes identified as his son. One day out hunting, the youth sights something he takes to be a wild beast; he tells Lamech and then guides Lamech who shoots the creature, only to discover that he has killed his ancestor Cain. In anger or sorrow or frustration—depending upon the variation of the legend—

Lamech then kills the youth. Though the details varied, common to most versions was the Cain-mistaken-for-a-wild-beast element, undeniably an emphasis on the dehumanized condition of Cain. It was this Lamech legend of the more general type that achieved almost semicanonical status in Christian exegesis and literature.[123] This long-lived theme did not appear in the visual arts until the eleventh century, but then it burst forth in three different areas: Byzantium,[124] Spain,[125] and Italy,[126] and its visual representation then continued and increased in subsequent centuries, as for example in the Bohun Psalter and the fresco at Pisa (figs. 1 and 3).

It is easy to see how the horn as Cain's mark could be incorporated into the Lamech story. And indeed their natural affinity was recognized and the two were combined, in the Tanhuma Midrash (one of several texts that have been described as containing essentially homiletic Midrashim). This text belongs to the era called the Middle Period (dating between the Muslim conquest and the end of the tenth century), and its final redaction has been dated as probably ninth century.[127] But since old and new materials are mixed together indiscriminately, it is difficult to date individual themes and interpretations. The Tanhuma Midrash combined the two legends—the horn as a mark of Cain, and Lamech killing Cain—by converting the Cain-the-wild-beast element in the Lamech legend into Cain-a-beastlike-man-with-a-horn. This version describes the youth as Lamech's son who reports: "Oh, father, you have killed something that resembles a man except it has a horn on its forehead!"[128]

Examples of the conflation of the horn of Cain legend with the Lamech legend are scarce. Yet there is evidence in art of the horn of Cain joined to the Lamech story. The Lamech legend—both with and without a horned Cain—may have been especially well known in France, at least in the area of Vézelay and Autun. At Vézelay the legend was carved twice: once for a capital of the nave, dated about 1120, and again for a capital in the narthex dated around 1140. It is the earlier version that includes the horn motif (fig. 7). Note that on the left Lamech is guided by the youth to shoot, while on the right, Cain is depicted peering through some vegetation. An antler-type of growth[129] emerges from his head as can be better seen in the enlarged detail (fig. 8). In neighboring Autun, also on a sculptured capital of the first half of the twelfth century, Cain has again been depicted with a horn in a representation of the Lamech story, but here with a different design for the horn (fig. 9), as best seen in the enlarged detail (fig. 10). These quite differently conceived horn styles at Vézelay and Autun suggest an oral transmission of the theme,[130] not a copying of visual models.

The horn carved at Autun at the side of Cain's head, as well as the antler-type of horn at Vézelay, suggest two horns rather than a single horn. One horn or two seems not to have mattered much in the transmittal of the legend. Both occur in two versions of an uncanonical Armenian Adambook, originally composed, possibly as early as the fourth century, but surely before the tenth.[131] In each of these Armenian versions the horn or horns have the startling feature of being able to speak.[132] One version mentions that the Lord inflicted seven punishments on Cain and that the first punishment was "that upon his head sprung up two horns."[133] The second punishment mentioned for Cain was:

that one of the horns cried out in a loud voice saying: "Cain is the murderer of his brother." And the mountains, the rocks and the valleys echoed saying: "Cain is the murderer of his brother."[134]

It is especially interesting to note that the horns of Cain in this text were combined with the trembling of Cain, for Cain's third punishment listed is: "that he quivered like a yew-tree in his feet, hands, and all his members."[135] Yet this Armenian text says nothing explicit about a mark or sign. Both the horns and the trembling are listed as punishments.

In another version of the Armenian Adambook the seven punishments that Cain was subjected to are listed in a different order, and a few other minor variations occur here and there. The fifth punishment is said to be: "Thou shalt quiver like a tree in the wind,"[136] and in this case a single horn is listed as Cain's seventh punishment:

Seventh: God put a sign upon him, that he might be recognized by every one; and the sign was a mark. A horn also grew out of his forehead; and wherever he went, the horn cried out with a loud voice, saying: "Cain, the murderer of his brother, is coming!"[137]

Note that although in the two-horned version nothing about a mark or sign was mentioned, in this one-horned version, part of Cain's seventh punishment is the sign that God put on him—a mark: "and the sign was a mark." But then the text continues, saying a horn also grew out of his forehead. It is the "also" that is confusing. Is the horn meant to be understood as something additional to the mark-sign, or is the horn the sign? These two Armenian texts demonstrate the kind of jumble that has so often permeated thought regarding Cain's curse, Cain's punishments, and Cain's mark. By now it should be evident that from time to time they were cleverly juggled so that curse, punishment, and mark were blended to be each and all simultaneously.

There is another interesting difference between the two Armenian versions. The text alluding to a one-horned Cain does not relate the horn to the Lamech legend, while the two-horned version does tie the horn motif to Cain's legendary death by Lamech, for later in that version we read:

And Lamech having mounted a horse, and gone hunting, Cain came in sight from afar with his horns and skin. [138] Lamech, on seeing him, thought it was a stag; and letting an arrow fly from his bow, he killed Cain. [139]

This is significant evidence for it shows us how varied the traditions were even in a single cultural tradition, for the horn of Cain appeared as an isolated theme in one of the Armenian Adambooks, but was tied to the Lamech legend in another.

The story of a horned Cain linked to his death by Lamech received especially explicit visual-artistic treatment in the fourteenth-century English Holkham Bible (with an Anglo-Norman text). [140] A taste for concrete and specific details is evident throughout this manuscript. A special kind of loving care has been lavished on the anecdotal elements of the stories, whether biblical or legendary. The Cain and Abel story (along with many apocryphal elements and legends) is elaborately portrayed on four and a half pages: the *Sacrifices of the brothers* (folio 5); the *Murder of Abel* and the *Lord cursing Cain* (folio 5v); *Cain and his evil brood* (folio 6); *Lamech killing Cain* (folio 6v); and *Lamech killing the youth* (the upper scene of folio 7). It is in the upper scene of folio 6v (fig. 11), where Lamech has just aimed his arrow at Cain, that an evil and grossly caricatured Cain is depicted wearing the horns of his curse-mark, as can be more clearly seen in the enlarged detail (fig. 12). Be assured. That is what they are. Nothing was left to chance in this manuscript. This is confirmed by the repetition of the same artistic design for the horns in the lower scene where Lamech is shown having just killed Cain. Cain lies dead at the right; the same distinctive curled horns protrude below the edge of his hood (detail, fig. 13). W. O. Hassall also noted the horns in his discussion of folio 6: "The hat conceals the mark of Cain, the two horns which are twice shown on the next page."[141] The Lamech story was extended and ended on the next page (folio 7). In the upper right (fig. 14) the youth discovers and identifies the victim (Cain). The artist has intentionally covered Cain's forehead by lowering his hood; the horns are no longer visible. At the left, the youth pointing to dead Cain, reports the catastrophe to Lamech who, in turn, angered by this disaster, proceeds to beat the boy to death with his bow.

The Lamech legend entered the province of Christian literature too,[142] and though it rarely contained the horned Cain motif, there are a few interesting examples. The combination of the two themes occurs, for example, in the *Lebor Gabála* (mentioned earlier with reference to beardlessness).[143] This poetic version contains a death of Cain by Lamech, but with an apple instead of the more common arrow:

After that seven wens took hold
upon Cain, after the kin-murder:
a wen [upon] each of his fair feet,
and two wens upon his hands.

A wen in his forehead, alas,
and a wen [upon] each of his cheeks:
through the wen of his forehead, very wretched!
[went] the apple which Lamech cast.

Lamech the two-spoused, without falsehood,
he is the first man who took two wives:
by him did crooked Cain fall,
after he cast the apple upon him.[144]

Note that here Cain's horn has been transformed into seven wens (lumps)—a little like warts—and the prose version in the *Lebor Gabála,* though it does not include the apocryphal story of Cain's demise, nevertheless repeats the seven wens for Cain:

God set Cain in a sign, so that no man should slay him—a lump upon his forehead (and a lump on each of his cheeks, and a lump on each foot and on each hand) and his being beardless, and being a fugitive.[145]

The combination of the Lamech legend and the horn of Cain received its most elaborate treatment in

Cornish drama. It was worked into a lengthy sequence in a play known as the *Creation of the World (Gwreans an Bys)*. [146] Some of the play's subject matter is indebted to an earlier Cornish play *Origo Mundi*, [147] and it is also possibly partly indebted to Breton plays where the language was Celtic, [148] but many of its stories and themes are totally different, including the legendary death of Cain. The text of the *Creation of the World* is Cornish, but with English stage directions. It is signed by a William Jordan (whose identity has remained unknown) and is dated August 12, 1611, but Jordan may only have been a transcriber, for the English forms in the stage directions have been described as earlier than 1611. [149] A Lamech sequence also appeared in that late medieval French play *Le mistère du viel Testament* discussed earlier, but there without a horned Cain; the youth sighting Cain refers to him only as "quelque sauvagine" (line 4724) or as a "beste" (line 4749). And there is a Lamech interlude in a play from the English *Ludus Coventriae* (another of the Corpus Christi cycles, also known as the N. Town cycle). But there too Cain is described by the youth only as a beast. [150] There is no mention of a horned Cain in either the French or the English Corpus Christi play. The infrequent appearance of the combined themes of Lamech killing Cain and a horned Cain in surviving evidence may not be a correct indicator of their past popularity. We are, after all, at the mercy of haphazard survivals. The inclusion of these combined themes in the Cornish play is of great importance, hinting that possibly a more vigorous life existed for them at an earlier time. Therefore the most pertinent sequences merit quotation. The marking of Cain is first mentioned when God the Father curses Cain and says:

A token on thee I will make—
When that shall be seen
　　　Thou shalt not be touched by a man.[151]

Then the English stage instructions follow which read:

Let the father make a marcke in his forehedd this word omega.[152]

There is nothing in the later part of the play, as we will see shortly, that is consistent with this earlier marking of Cain with an Omega. It is possible that the Cornish text was composed at some much earlier date and the English instructions are a later addition and intrusion to the expressions related to the mark of Cain later in the play. The really serious treatment of Cain's mark begins when Cain and Calmana (Cain's sister-wife according to legend) are discussing their departure. Cain says that he fears death (though allegedly protected by God), and wants to live in the woods to avoid discovery. Calmana then responds noting that the mark on Cain is a horn:

Therein thou art to blame:
　　　God hath set a mark on thee,
In the horn of thy forehead here
　　　And thus he said
　　　　These words right surely:—
Whatsoever man shall see that [i.e., his horn]
And shall slay thee,
　　　He shall have sevenfold more.[153]

Cain, however, is doubtful of the Lord's promise (and thus of the horn's protective value), and says:

For the promise I will not give an egg:
Trust him I will not,
    For fear of being deceived.[154]

And Cain insists that since everything is ready they and their small children must depart. A little later the playwright introduces the audience to Lamech and his servant who are preparing to go hunting. This is followed by a brief interlude where Cain describes himself and his exiled state to the audience. Cain is still unrepentant as he describes his cursed state:

By every one I am forgotten,
    I know not much people;
. . . .
Yet my heart is stout:
Because of slaying Abel (the) lout,
    Nor yet of the father's curse
        Have I repentance at all in (the world).[155]

Cain continues, commenting on his own deformed state. The element of hairiness has been added thereby heightening the image of a beastlike Cain:

Ye see me overgrown
    I am altogether with hair:
. . . .
        A son of curses I am made.
Through that I am not
        Come among people at any time;
    But always keeping myself
        In woods and in bushes,
        Like a beast ever living.[156]

Cain, emphasizing his distrust of God's protection, says that he will go and hide in some bush. It is at this point that the Lamech hunting scene resumes. Lamech's servant says that he sees a very large bullock and helps Lamech aim and shoot the alleged beast; then they approach to investigate what kind of bullock they have felled. Cain—not quite dead— laments his fate. Lamech hears him and is shocked for he realizes that he may have slain a man, not a beast, and reprimands his servant. The servant again stresses Cain's beastlike characteristics:

Hairy, quaint he is and ugly;
    I know not what beast it can be:
It should seem by his favour
        That he is some goblin of night
            And that shall be proved.[157]

Lamech approaches and questions stricken Cain, saying:

Who art thou? say to me
    If thou art a man or a great beast—
        A doubt of thee is to me.[158]

Cain reveals his identity as Lamech's ancestor and adds the information about his horned mark:

God's mark on me is set,
    Thou sees it in (the) horn of my forehead;
By man when it shall be discovered,
        With me certainly ought not
            To be meddled on any account.[159]

The playwright's interest in the theme is evident by the fact that he is not content to let it be, but repeats it: first by having Lamech ask:

Why did God set a mark
   In (the) horn of thy forehead?[160]

Then with Cain replying:

And His mark he set here
In (the) horn of my forehead for a token.[161]

After a great deal of agonized conversation, Cain dies. Lamech, true to legend, then dashes out the brains of his servant.

As I mentioned earlier, this elaborate sequence about Cain's horn in the Lamech episode may indicate popularity for the combined themes in earlier periods. But beyond the horn motif, the element of hairiness in this play deserves some further discussion, for though it is not designated as Cain's mark, it does indeed mark Cain. It is an element like beardlessness or like the horn since it suggests a blemish or disfigurement of the body. One of the uncanonical Armenian Adambooks discussed earlier introduced the idea of hairiness too, but obliquely, that is, by describing a horned Cain dressed with animal skins.[162] It too was an attempt to stress his beastlike state. Though there seems to be no really hairy Cain in medieval art, there was an attempt to portray his beastlike existence. This appears in a thirteenth-century Pamplona Bible,[163] where Cain is depicted with wild, disheveled hair, wearing a robe made of an animal skin in the scene of the *Lord cursing Cain* in the upper part of folio 6 verso (fig. 15), and again in the scene of *Lamech killing Cain* in the lower part of folio 7 recto.[164]

The visual representation of a hirsute Cain seems only to have been realized in the twentieth century

—an idea that was exploited by Gerhard Marcks in a woodcut of 1960 showing Cain killing Abel (fig. 16).[165] Marcks has, to be sure, represented Cain as hairy before he receives his curses or punishments or marks in the biblical text. Yet, this is not surprising, for artists (medieval and later) have frequently ignored correct biblical or other traditional sequences.[166]

What about the horn motif as Cain's mark independent of the Lamech legend? It appeared initially, as will be recalled, in the Genesis Rabbah, as one of seven different interpretations of the mark, and unconnected with any Lamech story.[167] It then appeared as an isolated motif in one of the two Armenian Adambooks, and again in the prose version (as contrasted with the poem) of the Irish *Lebor Gabála*.[168] It is fascinating to see the motif surface completely independent and unrelated to the Lamech story in a much earlier Irish text, the *Saltair na Rann*,[169] an Irish Adambook, dated end of the tenth century.[170] Cain's horn is again transformed into a wen as in the later *Lebor Gabála*—that is, into a lump on his forehead—but it is one, not seven. This text in fact may have been the precursor and model for the seven wens in the *Lebor Gabála*. In the *Saltair na Rann* (lines 1993–1996), God threatens the traditional sevenfold vengeance on anyone who would kill Cain, then immediately after, in lines 1997–2000 we read:

After that my bright King put the sign of guilt on Cain; so that the guilt would not be concealed, he put a lump on his forehead.[171]

Here Cain's horn serves more as an identifying and humiliating badge than as a protective device. A death of Cain is also described in the *Saltair na Rann*, but not at the hands of Lamech. Instead, Cain is killed in a bizarre incident or accident when a tree hits the lump on his forehead (lines 2001–4):

After that luckless Cain died one evening in the valley of Jehosaphat, when a bent tree struck firmly and strongly against the lump which was on his forehead.[172]

That the horn as the mark of Cain might have been more commonly popular than is presently evidenced is strengthened by the significant disavowal of it by Rupert of Deutz who coupled it with the interpretation of a trembling of the body that I mentioned earlier.

And the mark of Cain was not a trembling of the body, nor was it a horn that grew out of his forehead, for such notions come from Jewish tales and not from the authority of scripture.[173]

This emphatic denial by Rupert is convincing testimony of just how irresistible the horn legend may have been. While it is uncertain that the concept of the mark as a trembling of the body came from Jewish tradition (as I mentioned earlier), yet Jewish tradition is surely the original source for the horn; and Rupert himself was in a position to know at least some Jewish materials.[174]

The horn as a mark of Cain, independent of the Lamech legend, even emerged in the visual arts. I have located only one example thus far, but a most extraordinary specimen, in a thirteenth-century English psalter.[175] Three folios of this psalter are devoted to the biblical story of Cain and Abel. Yet, the psalter contains no representation of the Lamech story. On folio 5 verso (fig. 17) and folio 6 recto (fig. 18), the traditional depictions occur of *The Offerings of Cain and Abel,* and *Cain killing Abel.* It is on the very next folio, 6 verso (fig. 19) that the biblical account of Cain and Abel is completed. It portrays the cursing and the marking of Cain, here with these unusual, really quite astonishing black horns (enlargement on fig. 20). How amazing to see this ancient midrashic theme suddenly emerge in a thirteenth-century English psalter. Is this an isolated and lonely tip of what might have been a hidden mass of accumulated traditional lore? I would attribute this unique portrayal to the strangely wonderful, conservative ability of folklore to preserve and transmit ideas of former times.[176] There is in fact contemporary evidence that the belief that a horn (or horns) was Cain's mark still survives; it was recently described to me thus: "In the folklore of the Netherlands I have encountered the notion that a violent individual with a prominently developed brow—in particular the crescent-shaped area in the centre of the forehead and the two protrusions suggestive of rudimentary horns—carries the mark of Cain."[177] The horn motif never achieved the semicanonical status of the more general Lamech legend. Its appearances were erratic, and quite like folkloristic motifs in general, it seldom surfaced, at least not in the contexts where later historians can observe it. Yet it may have been commonly beloved in its secure underground shelter.

This depiction of Cain in the English psalter represents the emergence of more esoteric lore. Cain has

also been represented there with predominantly negroid features (figs. 19, 20). The cursing of Ham and
the cursing of Cain were the two favorite expla-
nations offered for the origin of the black races.[178]
Though black skin was more commonly ascribed to
Ham and his son (Canaan), Negroes were, in some
quarters, thought to have been descendants of Cain,
who was blackened by God, thus identifying the
mark of Cain with the blackness and the negroid features of the African races.[179] This is not the place to
describe in detail the practice of representing evil men
as dark-skinned or negroid, or both, in medieval
art.[180] But it is important in this case to emphasize
that in this English psalter, only one figure other than
Cain is depicted with negroid features—one of the
evil men who arrest Christ in the scene of the *Betrayal.* (See fig. 21 and enlarged detail in fig. 22.) The
representation of Cain in this English psalter with
two physical "blemishes"—horns and negroid
features—is, I believe, further evidence of what can
be called the medieval Englishman's extraordinary
taste for the explicit.

The concept of blackness (as the mark of Cain) can
also be traced in ancient Jewish sources, though not
directly associated with Genesis 4:15. It occurs in the
same Genesis Rabbah that has been referred to
throughout this study, but here with reference to the
sacrifices offered by Cain and Abel to the Lord. The
commentary states that Cain's face was blackened
when his offering was rejected by the Lord:

And Cain was very wroth (wayyiḥar) and his countenance
fell: [His face] became like a firebrand.[181]

"Firebrand" has been translated and explained as "blackened."[182] The influence of this midrashic interpretation on later thought can be demonstrated, for the same notion is expressed in one of the uncanonical Armenian Adambook texts. It occurs there too with reference to the sacrifices offered by the brothers where Cain's face is again blackened after his imperfect sacrifice has been rejected, but this time not by fire but by hail:

And the Lord was wroth with Cain, and as a handful of dust is carried away of the wind, so he scattered all his harvest of corn and destroyed all his riches, so that not even an ear of corn could be found. He beat Cain's face with hail, which blackened like coal, and thus he remained with a black face.[183]

Medieval, Renaissance, post-Renaissance and, unfortunately, post-post-post Renaissance minds have considered dark-skinned and negroid types, at the very least, savage and not quite human, associated them with devils and confused them with apes. Their occasional attribution to Cain was part of the tradition. No matter that all of Cain's descendants were supposed to have perished in the Flood.[184] The desire to emphasize the evil nature of Cain led to fabulous conceptions about his descendants, and among those ideas the notion that some of his progeny ultimately produced black children, as for example in the Middle High German poetical *Genesis* of the early twelfth century:

Some [children produced by the evil descendants of Cain] lost altogether their beautiful complexion; they became black and terrible, there was nothing like them.[185]

The belief in the very real survival of Cain's seed was not uncommon,[186] and until recently it lived on in Mormon theology. Joseph Smith published some of his revelations in a tract known as the *Pearl of Great Price*.[187] First in some visions of Moses allegedly revealed to Joseph Smith in June 1830, Smith established blackness as the mark of Cain. We read in the *Book of Moses*,[188] chap. 7:

verse 8:   . . . and there was a blackness came upon all the children of Canaan, that they were despised among all people.

and in verse 22:   And Enoch also beheld the residue of people which were the sons of Adam; and they were a mixture of all the seed of Adam save it was the seed of Cain, for the seed of Cain were black, and had not place among them.

Then in Joseph Smith's *Book of Abraham*,[189] which he claimed was a translation of an ancient papyrus found in Egypt and written by Abraham's own hand, Smith explained that Pharaoh and the Egyptians were descended from Cain and therefore could not hold the priesthood (*Abraham,* chap. 1: verses 21–22). The descent is described in verses 22–24:

verse 22:   From this descent sprang all the Egyptians, and thus the blood of the Canaanites was preserved in the land.

verse 23:   The land of Egypt being first discovered by a woman who was the daughter of Ham, and the daughter of Egypt, which in the Chaldean signifies Egypt, which signifies that which is forbidden.

verse 24:   When this woman discovered the land it was under water, who afterward settled her sons in it; and thus, from Ham sprang that race which preserved the curse in the land.

Joseph Smith's dogma advanced by the above verses thus asserted that all the Canaanites were blackened, that they were the seed of Cain, and from them sprang the Egyptians via Egyptus (a black Canaanite married to Ham), preserving a black race descended from both Cain and Ham. The resultant mixture of curses thus established that the mark of Cain was blackness (or negroid features or both). His doctrine served as support for slavery, it forbade intermarriage, and it denied the priesthood to blacks.

Smith's ideas, at least until very recently, have been continuously defended in the Mormon Church so that blacks have been denied the priesthood for 148 years. Some Mormons maintained Smith's position in their own writings, repeating his doctrines in similar or more drastic ways, as for example, Bruce R. McConkie,[190] John Stewart,[191] and John Lund.[192] Lund in fact included a lengthy section devoted to: "What was the Mark of Cain?"[193] He answered his own question by quoting one of his Mormon prophets, Brigham Young, saying: "President Brigham Young has told us that the mark of Cain was a 'black skin.'" Then Lund added: "However, it is not necessary to rely on this single statement to arrive at this same conclusion. There are numerous references made by both ancient and modern prophets that point to the fact that Cain was the father of the race that became known as Negroid."[194] Lund's exegesis continued with sections on: "Why did Cain receive the Mark?" and, "What was the Curse of

Cain?"[195] It was only as of June 9, 1978, that Mormon policy seems to have finally changed. It changed—so said church leaders—because of a "revelation given to the top leaders of the church."[196] What effect this declaration will have is still somewhat uncertain.

4

Intentionally Distorted Interpretations of Cain's Mark

Though a variety of interpretations of the mark of Cain have been reviewed here—some with positive associations, others wholly negative—none so far could be described as intentionally distorted. Bias is, to be sure, reflected in all the interpretations, but it is the slant, in each case, of a straightforward attempt on the part of the interpreter to elucidate the strange biblical silence. There are, however, at least two examples—one late medieval, the other modern—that can best be described as intentionally distorted interpretations of the mark of Cain. In these cases the interpreter has designed his interpretation to serve his own purpose—a self-conscious twisting to achieve personal ends. Clarification or elaboration of biblical text is not the primary goal; rather, biblical elements are used to enhance the interpreter's particular point of view about something he is critical of in his contemporary society.

This occurs in the English mystery play known as the Wakefield *Mactacio Abel*[1] (*The Killing of Abel*)—part of another of the Corpus Christi cycles. The Wakefield plays, also known as the Towneley plays —thirty-two in all—are preserved in a unique manuscript in the Huntington Library, San Marino, Cal-

ifornia. All but one have been described as being
written during the third quarter of the fifteenth century,[2] but this is a copy of what at that time comprised the latest collection of this Wakefield cycle.
The *Mactacio Abel* may in fact be an old play that was
revised, though this is uncertain.[3] The character of
Cain in the *Mactacio Abel* has a bold veracity and a
humanity that does not exist in any of the other
medieval plays and as one scholar put it, "If anyone is
distorted, it is not the comic Cain but Abel, who is
invariably and almost intolerably right. We are almost tempted to sympathize with Cain when he replies to Abel's chastisement, 'How long wilt thou me
appech [accuse] with thi sermonyng?'"[4] The talented
Wakefield playwright contemporized the biblical
story and used his unusual Cain in a social satire that
is effectively directed at certain legal abuses of the
period. His interpretation of Cain appears in this context; to our modern minds it seems a hidden guise,
implicitly rather than explicitly stated, though there is
no reason to conclude that it was hidden or oblique
for fifteenth-century audiences.

Just how ingeniously the playwright wove his
criticism into this religious drama, has recently been
studied by Bennett Brockman who analyzed exactly
which familiar legal processes were mocked.[5] He
pointed out that the biblical mark of Cain was transformed satirically into a kind of royal letter patent of
protection.[6] There is actually no mention of Cain's
mark in the play; after Cain has killed Abel we only
hear God's threat of vengeance on anyone who might
try to kill Cain:

DEUS.   Nay, Caym, it bese not so;
  I will that no man other slo [slay],
  For he that sloys [slays] the, yong or old,
  It shall be punyshid sevenfold.[7]

Cain is not reassured; in fact he expresses the urgent need to bury Abel fearing that his peers will see the corpse, suspect him, and kill him. And it is immediately following an exchange between Cain and his servant that Cain tells his servant that he wants him to remove Abel's body. Garcio is afraid to participate in this act, saying:

GARCIO.   Yey, bot for ferde [fear] of grevance,
  Here I the forsake;
  We mon haue a mekill myschaunce [We shall
        have mighty mischance]
  And the bayles [bailiffs] vs take.[8]

Cain says that he will give Garcio a "release," which brings a scornful reply:

CAYM.   A, syr, I cry you mercy! Seasse,
  And I shall make you a releasse.
GARCIO.   What, wilt thou cry my peasse
  Thrughout this land?[9]

To cry the king's peace was to proclaim that he was under the king's protection,[10] and this is precisely what Cain intends to do and does. As Cawley described it, "God's refusal to allow the murderer himself to be murdered in punishment for his crime (371–3) is twisted by Cain into a royal proclamation of pardon of the sort that every man in Wakefield must have heard."[11] It is thus in Cain's proclamation of peace (a thorough mockery of the king's proclamation) that he declares his own safe conduct. In other words, he provides himself and his servant with the declarations (and documents) that are needed to protect them from dangers and death.

Cain begins as a town crier, then is taunted by Garcio in brilliant, rhythmic counterpoint verse. Cain's proclamation not only echoes the "letters of protection" of that period but also reflects the even more notoriously abused "royal prerogatives of pardon," as Brockman pointed out.[12] If one reads only Cain's lines, the proclamation sounds like a straightforward pompous statement; his seriousness, however, is humorously undercut by Garcio's irreverent asides, a vigorous puncturing of Cain's self-inflated status: Cain thus cries the king's protection for Garcio and himself:

CAYM.   I command you in the kyngys nayme,
GARCIO.   And in my masteres, fals Cayme,
CAYM.   That no man at thame [them] fynd fawt [fault] ne blame, [meaning Garcio and Cain himself].
GARCIO.   Yey, cold rost is at my masteres hame [home].
CAYM.   Nowther [neither] with hym nor with his knafe [servant].
GARCIO.   What! I hope my master rafe! [What, I think my master does rave!]
CAYM.   For thay are trew [true] full manyfold.
GARCIO.   My master suppys no coyle bot cold. [sups but cabbage cold.]
CAYM.   The kyng wrytys you vntill. [The king writes this to you of his will.]
GARCIO.   Yit ete I neuer half my fill.
CAYM.   The kyng will that thay be safe.

GARCIO.　Yey, a draght of drynke fayne wold I hayfe. [A draft of drink fain would I have.]

CAYM.　At thare awne will let tham wafe. [On their own let them fare and not grieve.]

GARCIO.　My stomak is redy to receyfe.

CAYM.　Loke no man say to theym, on nor other— [Make sure that no man say to them, one or the other]

GARCIO.　This same is he that slo [slew] his brother.

CAYM.　Byd euery man thaym [them] luf [love] and lowt [revere].[13]

Cain interrupts his protection proclamation to threaten Garcio, but then continues to proclaim the king's protection for all who attend the play, telling Garcio:

> Byd euery man theym pleasse to pay.

and forcing Garcio to continue, who addresses the audience thus:

GARCIO.　Now old and yong, or that ye weynd,
　　　[attended the play]
　The same blissyng withoutten end,
　All sam [altogether] then shall ye haue,
　That God of heuen my master has giffen.[14]

Cain crying his own peace thus establishes his own protection by the king's letter: The King writes this to you of his will; and by the king's pardon: The King wills that they be safe. It is of course uncertain whether or not any particular king and period of time has been satirized in this play. A letter of protection was available in the late fourteenth and fifteenth century for a price, but was looked upon as a relatively mild judicial abuse.[15] But the royal prerogative of pardon was often greatly abused; nine protests have been recorded during the fourteenth century,[16] as for example the disapproval evidenced in a Parliament petition of 1390 protesting that charters of pardon have been granted too lightly.[17] The Cain sequences in the *Mactacio Abel* are related in general to this kind of social climate; the audience would have certainly realized that the royal pardon Cain parodies made him and any other holders of such a pardon secure. The humor in this drama (outrageous or lively, depending on the viewpoint of the critic), may nevertheless be difficult to assess, but the cunning transformation of Cain's biblical mark into social satire is clear. Some scholars have understood it as a transformation of satire into profound theological dogma,[18] yet I think it could be viewed as theological dogma transmuted into social protest, and conceivably along with large chunks of religious doubt and disbelief.

The unusual interpretation of the mark that we saw in the Wakefield *Mactacio Abel* is probably unique in medieval life. I know of no other intentionally distorted interpretations of Cain's mark in the life of the Middle Ages or Renaissance. There is, however, an intentionally distorted Cain story told by Erasmus that ought to be mentioned, for it demonstrates that occasionally men could, and did, boldly depart from traditional approaches to evil Cain. Erasmus created a somewhat surprising story to distract some friends— theologians and lawyers entertained at dinner in Oxford by John Colet—who had become overheated by their discussion of the nature of Cain's sin. Erasmus himself preserves the story in his letter to John Sixtin.

Erasmus's fantasy version has Cain approaching and enticing and cleverly convincing the guardian angel of Paradise to distribute a few of the superb seeds of Eden. Cain plants them and produces such an abundant harvest that God is enraged, and out of jealousy plagues Cain with ants, weasels, toads, caterpillars, birds, mice, locusts, hailstorms, and tornados. The angel is punished by imprisonment in a human body and Cain's attempt to propitiate God with a burnt offering of fruits is refused. This sacrilegious approach to Cain was, of course, supposed to have been but a sham (though of course we can't be sure) for Erasmus ends his letter by saying:

This, Sixtinus, was the story that was told over our cups, and which had its birth among them and out of them, if you please. I have chosen to relate it to you, first, that I might have something to write, as I owed you a letter, and next, that you might not be altogether excluded from so dainty a banquet. Farewell. Oxford, [1499].[19]

The most intentionally distorted interpretation of Cain's mark appears in the twentieth century. It is appropriate for discussion here because it mirrors older traditions and ancient meanings, yet through a twisting of the story it projects an image that could only have been produced in the modern world. This is the bizarre interpretation that appears in the short novel, *Demian,* written by Hermann Hesse in 1919. It proceeds with a discussion between the young boy, Emil Sinclair, and the older hero, Demian. They have just finished listening to the traditional story of Cain and Abel in their school classroom and Demian suggests that there is quite a different interpretation possible, saying:

For instance, one can't be quite satisfied with this Cain and the mark on his forehead, with the way it's explained to us . . .

We can guess—no, we can be quite certain—that it was not a mark on his forehead like a postmark—life is hardly ever as clear and straightforward as that. It is much more likely that he struck people as faintly sinister, perhaps a little more intellect and boldness in his look than people were used to. This man was powerful: you would approach him only with awe. He had a "sign." You could explain this any way you wished. . . . So they did not interpret the sign for what it was—a mark of distinction—but as its opposite.[20]

Sinclair then questions Demian about the slaying of Abel and Demian suggests that the story was simply a rumor; however, he says that part of it was true, namely that:

Cain and his children really bore a kind of mark and were different from most people.[21]

Or, says Demian, if the story were true, it may just have been that a strong man slew a weaker one and "perhaps it was a valiant act, perhaps it wasn't." Demian explains that all the weaker ones were afraid of Cain from then on and complained, but because they were cowards they just said that they couldn't kill Cain because "he has a sign. God has marked him." Much later in the story, the two young men have grown up, and Sinclair has lost touch with Demian for the moment, but out on a walk, Sinclair says to himself:

During that walk I felt for the first time the mark of Cain on my forehead.[22]

Not too much later Sinclair is reunited with his friend. Sinclair asks Demian:

Did you recognize me at once?[23]

Demian replies, saying that of course he recognized Sinclair:

Of course. You've changed somewhat. But you have the sign.[24]

Sinclair replies:

The sign. What kind of sign?[25]

Then Demian explains:

We used to call it the mark of Cain earlier on—if you can still remember. It's our sign. You've always had it, that's why I became your friend. But now it has become more distinct.[26]

Sinclair is now welcomed into Demian's circle of friends and into the secret of those who wear the sign in their faces. Hesse then tells his readers the significance of the sign through the initiate, Sinclair:

We who wore the sign might justly be considered "odd" by the world; yes, even crazy, and dangerous. We were *aware* or in the process of becoming aware and our striving was directed toward achieving a more and more complete state of awareness while the striving of the others was a quest aimed at binding their opinions, ideals, duties, their lives and fortunes more and more closely to those of the herd . . . .

But whereas we, who were marked, believed that we represented the will of Nature to something new, to the individualism of the future, the others sought to perpetuate the status quo. [27]

Hesse, with philosophical reasons of a political kind, attempted a reconstruction or rehabilitation of Cain, converting Cain's mark into a sign of distinction. Those who have it are to a certain extent still outcasts (like ancient Cain); but with Hesse's imprint on them, they are the outsiders with inside knowledge:

Everywhere, he said, we could observe the reign of the herd instinct, nowhere freedom and love. All this false communion—from the fraternities to the choral societies and the nations themselves—was an inevitable development, was a community born of fear and dread, out of embarrassment, but inwardly rotten, outworn, close to collapsing. [28]

Those with Cain's sign, according to Hesse, are thus the men and women with gifted insight; they are the ones who can read the signs of the times. Though Hesse's construction is thoroughly modern, having moved far beyond the nihilistic depiction by Byron, it is strikingly unconvincing. His interpretation of the mark of Cain is so far removed from the imagery historically associated with the evil Cain that the wrenching produces puerile effects rather than an artistically successful distortion. For even though modern intellectuals view the biblical story as myth, the archetypal story of brother-murder is still too much a real part of our society to be treated so superficially. Though surely Hesse did not intend a shallow interpretation, that is what I find is the result of his attempt. It shows neither the artistic talent of a Wakefield playwright, nor the charming irreverence and sharp wit of an Erasmus.

5
Cain's Mark and the Jews

Little interest in the precise characteristics of Cain's mark was evidenced by the early church fathers, as I mentioned at the beginning of this study. Augustine, quite in keeping with this outlook, similarly showed little or no concern with the literal meaning of Cain's sign. He did, however, see substantial significance in its symbolism and he used it to form an integral part of an allegory on Cain and the Jews. Augustine's interpretation could be viewed as part of the category just discussed—distorted interpretations of the mark of Cain. Yet that would be simplistic; with that kind of approach all allegorical and typological comparisons could be viewed as intentionally distorted interpretations. An unflattering and odious comparison between Cain and the Jews was made by Ambrose, who if not the first to do so, was surely the first to state it so fully, so emphatically, and so succinctly, in his tract on Cain and Abel,[1] written about A.D. 375. Ambrose, indebted to Philo for his allegorical method, and for most of his ideas about Cain and Abel, updated and Christianized Philo's exegesis by inserting a bold typological comparison of Cain and the Jews. He stated unequivocally that murderer Cain was the prototype of the Jews:

These two brothers, Cain and Abel, have furnished us with the prototype of the Synagogue and the Church. In Cain we perceive the parricidal people of the Jews, who were stained with the blood of their Lord, their Creator, and as a result of the childbearing of the Virgin Mary, their Brother, also. By Abel we understand the Christian who cleaves to God.[2]

What Ambrose so compactly expressed, Augustine a little later extended and amplified with elaborate detail in his tract against Faustus and the Manichaeans.[3] In summary and outline fashion, Augustine's comments were expressed like this:

—As Cain's offering was rejected, so too the Old Testament observances are rejected;

—Abel the younger brother was killed by the elder; so too Christ, head of the younger people, is killed by the elder people—the Jews;

—Cain's ignorance when questioned by the Lord was pretended; likewise, the Jews deceive in their refusal of Christ;

—Just as Abel's blood accused Cain, so the blood of Christ accuses the Jews;

—As Cain was cursed from the earth, so the unbelieving Jews are cursed from the Holy Church;

—As Cain was punished to be a mourner and an abject on the earth, so too are the Jews;

—Cain was not punished with bodily death, so too the preservation of the Jews will be a proof to believing Christians of the merited subjection of the Jews;

—And last, but of special importance here, is Augustine's commentary on the mark which I quote in full:

And the Lord God set a mark upon Cain, lest any one finding him should slay him. It is a most notable fact, that all the nations subjugated by Rome adopted the heathenish ceremonies of the Roman worship; while the Jewish nation, whether under Pagan or Christian monarchs, has never lost the sign of their law, by which they are distinguished from all other nations and peoples. No emperor or monarch who finds under his government the people with this mark kills them, that is, makes them cease to be Jews, and as Jews to be separate in their observances, and unlike the rest of the world. Only when a Jew comes over to Christ, he is no longer Cain, nor goes out from the presence of God, nor dwells in the land of Naid, which is said to mean commotion.[4]

Augustine's ideas reverberated through the Middle Ages and in fact they increased in vigor as the centuries passed, finding a solid place in subsequent Christian exegesis. Bede, the English exegete mentioned earlier in this study, for example, repeats Augustine almost word for word.[5] But Isidore of Seville (ca. 560–636) though indebted to Augustine for all the basic ideas, spelled out in concrete language what Augustine had only indicated by suggestion, that the sign of the Jews is circumcision:

gens autem Judaeorum sive paganis regibus, sive sub Christianis, non amiserit signum legis, et circumcisionis suae, quo a caeteris gentibus populisque distinguitur.[6]

[But the Jewish people, whether under pagan or Christian kings, have not lost the sign of the law and of their circumcision, by which they are distinguished from other nations and peoples.]

The same words, "et circumcisionis suae," appear in Rabanus Maurus's exegesis,[7] while Remigius of Auxerre, though true to Augustinian herd instinct, did not follow the Isidorian departure spelling out precisely what the sign of the law was. There is no mention of circumcision. Remigius added, however, that the sign of the Jews led to their damnation but to "our" [Christian] rescue:

Allegorice posuit Deus signum in Judaeos, ut nemo eos occideret ipsam videlicet legem quam portabant ad suam damnationem et nostram ereptionem. Propter hoc signum nemo eos occidit. Neque enim pagana persecutione, vel etiam sub Christiana jam tranquilitate eos prohibuit suis legibus uti et suo more vivere.[8]

By the time we reach Bruno of Asti (ca. 1049–1123) the language has changed somewhat, but Bruno's basic ideas are those of Isidore and Rabanus Maurus:

Judaeis quoque circumcisionis signum a Domino datum est, quo a cunctis gentibus discernuntur, et qui cunctis gentibus subditi sunt, semperque timori et despectui dediti, nemo est qui occidere eos velit.[9]

[To the Jews too a sign, of circumcision, was given by the Lord, by which they are separated from all peoples, and there is no one who would want to kill those who have been subjected to all peoples and who have been exposed to fear and scorn.]

Recall that both Peter Comestor and Peter Riga a little later gave Cain a trembling head as his mark. Comestor, however, said that his head trembled because Cain had killed the head of the Church [Abel]—a rather neat comparison: a head for a head! He said nothing more, however, about Cain's mark as compared with the mark of the Jews. But Peter Riga, though indebted to Comestor for the interpre-

tation of Cain's mark as a movement of the head, in
contrast to Comestor, goes on to repeat the old Augustinian allegorical comparison. But in his own in-
imitable style, for he goes beyond the language of Isidore and the others, dwelling on the particulars of the
sign of the Jews, and spelling out the precise meaning
of circumcision:

Ira superna Cain dat signum ne perimatur:
    Signum ne perimi possit Hebreus habet.
Reuera satis est istud mirabile, mundo
    In mediis uiuit hostibus ille suis;
Nullus rex necat hunc, nullus dux, nulla potestas;
    Pro signo cunctis est resecata cutis.
Inter Christicolas et gentes spirat Hebreus;
    Non hunc occidit illa uel illa manus. [10]

[Divine wrath gives Cain a sign so that he
    will not be killed:
The Hebrew has a sign so that he cannot be killed.
In truth, that he lives on earth in the midst
    of his enemies is rather amazing.
No king, no duke, no powerful person kills him.
His skin has been cut as a sign to everyone.
The Hebrew lives among Christians and pagans;
Neither the one hand nor the other slays him.]

The commentaries and Riga's poem, *Aurora*, are
primarily theological documents. But by the twelfth
century, in the writings of Peter the Venerable, the
comparison of Cain and the Jews implies something
more contemporary; theological niceties are becoming increasingly sociological expressions. [11] And in
the thirteenth century, Innocent III brazenly applies
the theological concepts to medieval contemporary

Jews in his letter to the Count of Nevers I mentioned earlier, which I quote again, but in greater length:

> The Lord made Cain a wanderer and a fugitive over the earth, but set a mark upon him, making his head to shake, lest any finding him should slay him. Thus the Jews, against whom the blood of Jesus Christ calls out, although they ought not be killed, lest the Christian people forget the Divine Law, yet as wanderers ought they to remain upon the earth, until their countenance be filled with shame and they seek the name of Jesus Christ, the Lord.[12]

But that was in 1208. By 1215 Innocent III had promulgated the infamous decree—canon 68—at the Fourth Lateran Council where Jews (and Saracens) were required to distinguish themselves from Christians.[13] This is not to suggest that Christians were the first to separate believers from nonbelievers. This seems to have occurred first in Islam where special clothing and badges were designated for both Jews and Christians from about A.D. 634.[14] Though the means for such distinction in Christian lands was not spelled out, the Lateran decree clearly suggested a distinction in their clothing.[15] It was of course interpreted in different ways in various countries.[16] The Church did not prescribe any definite sign for the Jews to wear, but it often consisted of a special color of cloth in a distinctive shape on a part of the clothing.[17] Enormous financial gains from fines for not wearing a badge on the one hand, plus the sale of the badges on the other hand, helped win status for the denigrating badges in medieval life with relatively little opposition.[18] Innocent III himself, however, realized the danger of his own decree, and in a letter of about 1215–1216 stated:

The order is given them to let the Jews wear clothes by which they might be distinguished from Christians, but not to force them to wear such as would lay them open to the danger of loss of life.[19]

Medieval badges on Jews did not serve as protection; rather they served to identify and denigrate them. In England Jews were ordered to wear the two biblical tablets of the Law[20] in their diptych shape as the Jewish badge—even on a journey. The degradation that accompanied the Jewish badges of the Middle Ages and Renaissance is well known;[21] only in Spain, Portugal, and Italy, were the Jews able to resist the humiliating badge laws with moderate success for a time.[22] It seems that only with the seventeenth century did a fairer attitude begin to emerge,[23] and by the eighteenth century some enlightened progress was achieved.[24] But the modern badge laws of Nazi Germany[25] are firm and grim reminders of the institution that began officially with Innocent III in the thirteenth century, but whose real genesis can be laid to Augustine and his ancient allegorical comparison of Cain and the Jews—and more specifically to his comparison of the "sign" of the Jews and Cain's unknown, mysterious mark.

Summary

The interpretations discussed in this book were grouped together by genre: Cain himself identified as the mark or sign; an event designated as the mark; and, the greatest number of interpretations, those associated with Cain's body. The latter were characterized as a mark on Cain's body (as for example, a letter from the Lord's name), a movement of Cain's body (trembling of his limbs or a shaking of Cain's head), and blemishes associated with his body (beardlessness, leprosy, horn or horns, and blackness of the skin). In addition, a few interpretations reflected intentionally distorted viewpoints, while another type, the allegorical Augustinian interpretation comparing Cain's mark with the "mark" of the Jews had long-lasting implications, stretching through Christian exegesis, and symbolically finding a possible final resting place in the grim badges imposed on Jews by Nazi Germany.

Surprising patterns appear once the mass of those interpretations is scrutinized. Especially striking is the lack of interest in the nature of the mark evidenced by some of the early Jewish and Christian exegetes such as Philo, Josephus, Ambrose, Jerome, and Basil the Great. (Detailed specifics about the mark came from other quarters, as for example the seven different interpretations in the Genesis Rabbah.) Lack of concern about the characteristics of the mark on the part of those eminent early commentators may possibly help explain another of the historical surprises—the infrequent appearance of detailed information about the mark in literature and drama, and the astonishingly few representations of the mark, or the marking of Cain, in the visual arts. Ideas and themes elaborately expounded in early Jewish and Christian exegesis frequently did appear in literature and art but often not until much later. In the visual arts there is in fact an explosion of some of those themes in the eleventh and twelfth centuries, especially in northwestern Europe. The absence of concrete details about the mark of Cain in those early writers may provide a partial explanation for the rare appearance of details about the mark in literature, and for the infrequent representation of the theme in the visual arts.

Yet the sparse evidence that has remained—especially in drama and in the visual arts—is highly significant, for those chance survivals have preserved some of the major and minor interpretations in distinctive and sometimes detailed forms. The interpretation that Cain's mark was a trembling of the limbs had established itself rather early in Christian exegesis and thus its persistence in exegesis and its appearance in drama is not unexpected. Far more extraordinary is the long life of interpretations that did not achieve canonical status. The horn as the mark of Cain managed to survive, surfacing in unexpected places and periods: in early Armenian uncanonical texts; in an early tenth-century Irish Adambook; in twelfth-century French sculptured capitals; and in illuminations in thirteenth- and fourteenth-century English manuscripts. Its tenacious vigor as an idea was demonstrated by its extensive treatment in a late Cornish play. Blackness of skin and negroid features as the mark of Cain led an even more astonishing underground life. It appeared earliest in the Genesis Rabbah, turned up in one of the versions of the Armenian Adambook, appeared in an illumination in a thirteenth-century English psalter (combined with the horn motif), and thrived in the theology and practice of the Mormon religion.

There has been no consensus about the mark of Cain. We have seen how interpretations frequently ranged and changed in the early period depending upon whether it was believed to be a symbol of God's pardon or a symbol of condemnation. It could denote divine forgiveness, thus suggesting that the mark was a positive and protective device. But most often the mark, though protective, also denoted punishment. It functioned simultaneously as condemnation-curse and taboo-protection. Yet another category of interpretations presented viewpoints where Cain's mark had lost all of its protective qualities and had become only and wholly the shameful stigmatic identification of a criminal—the viewpoint that has remained the commonplace of today.

The multiple interpretations of the mark of Cain have indeed filled the biblical lacuna with a continuous and changing panorama of images. They were all meant to enlighten and instruct, and some were even intended to "entertain"—as in the Wakefield play or in Hesse's novel, and fantasy played a role in all of them. But beyond that the varied interpretations do enlarge our view of mankind; they disclose the re-markable creativity of men, who structuring concepts on slim or no evidence, reveal to us their resourceful talents and determined minds.

Notes

INTRODUCTION

1. The Kenites were a large group of nomadic tribes engaged in metal working. The root *qyn* has the same meaning in cognate Semitic languages (i.e., Arabic, Syriac, and Aramaic) and the proper noun, Tubal-Cain, a descendant of Cain who made implements of metal (Genesis 4:22), is a compound name in which the second noun indicated the trade. The connection between Cain and the Kenites has been most extensively argued by Bernhard Stade, "Das Kainszeichen," *Zeitschrift für die alttestamentliche Wissenschaft,* 14 (1894), 250–318. For a brief account of the Kenites and additional bibliography, see *Encyclopedia Judaica* (Jerusalem, 1971), under *Kenites.* Some scholars, however, view this theory of Cain as the eponymous ancestor of the Kenites as very doubtful; see for example, G. M. Landes, *The Interpreter's Dictionary of the Bible* (Nashville and New York, 1962), under *Kenites.*

2. The passage reads: "From Cain was descended Jethro, the father-in-law of Moses, as it is written, 'And the sons of the Kenite the father-in-law of Moses,' and according to tradition he was called Kenite because he originated from Cain." See *The Zohar,* trans. Harry Sperling and Maurice Simon, 5 vols., 1st ed. 1934 (London, Jerusalem, New York, reprint of 1973), Zohar I, 28a, vol. 1, p. 108. The Zoharic commentary derived from Judges 1:16 which reads (translation from the Hebrew Masoretic text [Philadelphia: Jewish Publication Society of America, 1917]):

"And the children of the Kenite Moses' father-in-law,
went up out of the city of palm-trees . . ." The Zohar
commentator's conclusion that Jethro was descended from
Cain evolved not from sophisticated etymological-histor-
ical analysis, but rather from assonances, i.e., similari-
ties of sounds between Kenite and Cainite (of Cain). This
Zoharic commentary is interesting since on the one hand
it appears to approach some of the concepts of modern biblical source criticism, yet on the other hand it posits a literal interpretation that would make all the descendants of
Moses (through his wife Zipporah, daughter of Jethro) descendants of Cain (no matter that Cain's line was supposed
to have completely perished in the flood).

3. The enormous complexity of this undertaking can be
rapidly grasped by perusing the great work of Otto
Eissfeldt, *The Old Testament, The History of the Formation of
the Old Testament*, trans. Peter R. Ackroyd (1965) from the
3d German ed. of 1964 (1st German ed., 1934) (New York,
Evanston, San Francisco, London, reprint of 1974).

4. For example the Samaritan Pentateuch, the Targums,
the Peschitta and other Syriac translations, the Septuagint,
the translations of Aquila, Theodotion and Symmachus,
the *Vetus Latina*, and the Vulgate. There are summaries of
these and bibliographies in the Eissfeldt book cited above;
see pp. 694–719, and additional literature and notes on pp.
782–785.

5. Biblical citations and quotations throughout this
study are from the Vulgate (or the Douay translation) un-
less otherwise stated.

6. This is the interpretation offered by Philo, see below,
pp. 14–15, and much later by Rupert of Deutz, see below,
p. 51.

7. Sometimes the sign is designated as an event that
takes place; see below, p. 20, and Chap. 2, n. 18.

1. CAIN AND REPENTANCE

1. See John Bowker, *The Targums and Rabbinic Literature* (Cambridge, 1969), pp. 3–14 and Martin McNamara, *The New Testament and the Palestinian Targum to the Pentateuch* (Rome, 1966), pp. 38–41.

2. Bowker, *The Targums and Rabbinic Literature*, p. 3.

3. Ibid., p. 8.

4. Ibid., p. 14.

5. McNamara, *The New Testament and the Palestinian Targum to the Pentateuch.*

6. Bowker, *The Targums and Rabbinic Literature*, p. 15.

7. Translations of the Masoretic text throughout this study are from *The Holy Scriptures* (Philadelphia: Jewish Publication Society of America, 1917). For the purpose of this study, I have used this 1917 translation rather than the one of 1962 because the earlier translation preserves the subtle ambiguity of the original. At Genesis 4:15, the 1962 translation reads: "And the LORD put a mark on Cain lest anyone who met him should kill him." The 1917 translation reads: "And the LORD set a sign for Cain lest any finding him should smite him." A "sign for Cain" may or may not be a "mark on Cain," and thereon hangs much of the interpretive tale. This ambiguity has been the portal through which, again and again, interpreters' dreams have escaped into and out of the text (cf. the discussion of Midrash Genesis Rabbah below). For that reason, it should be preserved in translation.

8. See the discussion by Geza Vermes, "The Targumic Versions of Genesis IV 3–16," *The Annual of Leeds University Oriental Society,* 3 (1961–62), 81–114, and especially 103–104.

9. Bowker, *The Targums,* p. 21.

10. Ibid., translation, p. 135.

11. Ibid., p. 26.

12. Ibid., translation, p. 133.

13. See Vermes, "The Targumic Versions of . . . ," p. 104.

14. Bowker, *The Targums,* pp. 22–26.

15. See article in the *Encylopedia Judaica* (Jerusalem, 1971), under *Targum*; and see Bowker, *The Targums,* pp. 22–23.

16. Bowker, *The Targums,* translation, p. 135.

17. I am indebted to Carol Lanham for this translation—as well as for other translations of Greek and Latin throughout this study.

18. Josephus (*Jewish Antiquities,* I, 2, 1); see trans. H. St. J. Thackeray (London and New York, 1930), 4:27.

19. Ibid., p. 29.

20. See *The Latin Josephus,* ed. Franz Blatt (Copenhagen, 1957), Introduction, p. 12, and for the appropriate Latin text see pp. 130–131.

21. See Bowker, *The Targums,* pp. 45–46.

22. *The Midrash Rabbah,* ed. and trans. H. Freedman and Maurice Simon, 10 vols. (London, 1939), foreword by I. Epstein, p. xviii; and see Hermann L. Strack, *Introduction to the Talmud and Midrash,* orig. ed. 1931 (New York, repr. 1969), pp. 201–203.

23. *The Midrash Rabbah,* p. xix.

24. Ibid., pp. xx–xxi.

25. See *Encyclopedia Judaica,* under *Midrash.*

26. Bowker, *The Targums,* p. 79.

27. *The Midrash Rabbah,* Bereshith XXII:13, pp. 191–192.

28. Ibid., p. 191.

29. Bowker, *The Targums,* p. 64.

30. See *The Babylonian Talmud,* ed. and trans. Isidore Epstein and Maurice Simon, 18 vol. ed. (London, 1961), Seder Nezikin, Sanhedrin 37b, III:237 and n. 7.

31. Bowker, *The Targums*, p. 85.

32. Ibid.

33. *Pirķê de Rabbi Eliezer* (*The Chapters of Rabbi Eliezer the Great*), introd. and trans. Gerald Friedlander, 1st ed. 1916 (New York, reprint of 1970), p. 155, editor's n. 8.

34. For the full quotation, see ibid., pp. 155–156. Friedlander dates the final redaction around the second or third decade of the ninth century. This late date does not, however, mean that most of its material is this late; in fact much of it goes back to earlier periods. See introduction, pp. liii–lv, for a discussion of the dating.

35. See Gershom Scholem, *Kabbalah* (Jerusalem, 1974), p. 233.

36. Ibid., pp. 222–226.

37. *The Zohar*, trans. Harry Sperling and Maurice Simon, 5 vols., 1st ed. 1934 (London, Jerusalem, New York, reprint of 1973), Zohar I, 54b, vol. 1, p. 173.

38. See Vermes, "The Targumic Versions of Genesis IV 3–16," pp. 104–105.

2. EARLY EXEGESIS

1. Philo, English trans. F. H. Colson and G. H. Whitaker, Loeb Classical Library, 10 vols. and 2 suppl. vols., 1st ed., 1929 (Cambridge, Mass. and London, reprint of 1968), *The Worse Attacks the Better*, sections 177–78, II:319.

2. Ibid.

3. *Jewish Antiquities*, I, 1, 1, trans., p. 29.

4. Philo, *Questions and Answers on Genesis*, Loeb Classical Library, Supplement 1, trans. Ralph Marcus (Cambridge, Mass., 1953), p. 45; Josephus, *Jewish Antiquities*, I, 2, 1. trans. p. 29

5. Philo, *Questions and Answers on Genesis*, p. 45.

6. Saint Ambrose, *Hexameron, Paradise, and Cain and Abel*, trans. John Savage (New York, 1961), Fathers of the

Church, 42:433. For the Latin see, *Sancti Ambrosii Opera,* ed. Carolus Schenkl, *Corpus Scriptorum Ecclesiasticorum Latinorum, De Cain et Abel,* 32/1 (Vienna-Prague-Leipzig, 1897), 406.

7. *De Cain et Abel, CSEL,* p. 406.

8. *Cain and Abel,* trans. John Savage, p. 432.

9. *De Cain et Abel, CSEL,* p. 406.

10. *Cain and Abel,* trans. John Savage, p. 434.

11. The worst kind of punishment might easily be the long-enduring or eternal punishment; see the interesting comments on this theme by George K. Anderson, *The Legend of the Wandering Jew* (Providence, R.I., 1965), pp. 2–10.

12. In Jerome's Letter no. 36, *Ad Damasum,* sect. 2; see Saint Jerome, *Lettres,* 8 vols., ed. and trans. Jérôme Labourt, Latin and French on parallel pages, Tome II (Paris, 1951), p. 53: Jerome in fact stated that Cain was later killed in the seventh generation by his descendant, Lamech (section 4, p. 54), a legendary account of Cain's death of Jewish origin that achieved great popularity in both Jewish and Christian circles (to be discussed later).

13. Ibid., p. 54.

14. Saint Basil, *Collected Letters,* trans. Roy Joseph Deferrari, Loeb Classical Library, 4 vols. (London and Cambridge, Mass., 1926–1934), vol. 4, Letter 260, pp. 49–73, especially pp. 59–63.

15. Letter 260, p. 63; and see Deferrari's appendix, "The Interpretations of Genesis 4:15," discussed in Letter 260, pp. 359–361.

16. *Midrash Rabbah,* 1:191.

17. Abraham Levene has analyzed this passage and has dated some of its elements in his *The Early Syrian Fathers on Genesis* (London, 1951), p. 169.

18. Louis Ginzberg pointed out that another event was offered as interpretation in a later text, namely, that the

Sabbath—the sign between God and Israel (Exod. 31:13) —came in and saved Cain from death, *Legends of the Jews*, 5 vols., 1st ed. 1925 (Philadelphia, reprint of 1947), 5:141, n. 28. The idea of an event as a sign is most clearly demonstrated by God's rainbow as a sign of a covenant between God and the earth and its inhabitants (Gen. 9:12–17).

19. This idea was obliquely suggested by Philo, see above, p. 15, later by Rupert of Deutz, see below, p. 51.

3. THE MARK ASSOCIATED WITH CAIN'S BODY

1. *New Schaff-Herzog Encyclopedia of Religious Knowledge*, 13 vols. (New York and London, 1908), vol. 2, under *Cain, Kenites.*

2. *New Catholic Encyclopedia,* 15 vols. (New York, 1967), vol. 2, under *Cain and Abel.*

3. Tikva Frymer-Kensky, "The Atrahasis Epic and its Significance for our Understanding of Genesis 1–9," *Biblical Archeologist* (Dec., 1977), p. 153. She repeated the error in a later version of this same article, "What the Babylonian Flood Stories can and cannot teach us about the Genesis Flood," *Biblical Archaeology Review* (Nov.–Dec., 1978), p. 39.

4. Franz Dölger, *Sphragis. Eine altchristliche Taufbezeichnung in ihren Beziehungen zur profanen und religiösen Kultur des Altertums* [Studien zur Geschichte und Kultur des Altertums, Fünfter Band. 3./4. Heft]. (Paderborn, 1911).

5. See for example the following: Alice Morse Earle, *Curious Punishments of Bygone Days* (Chicago, 1896), chapter on branding and maiming, pp. 138–149; Harry Elmer Barnes, *The Story of Punishment* (Boston, 1930), p. 62; Hans Fehr, *Das Recht im Bilde* (Erlenbach-Zürich, 1923), 1:106 and the illustration (fig. 137, p. 85) of 1817 showing Kaspar Meyer of Bern—convicted of robbery—being publicly branded on his forehead.

6. See Steven Runciman, *The Medieval Manichee*, 1st ed. 1947 (Cambridge, 2d ed. 1960), who speaks of "the regular penalties of branding and exile," p. 99; and see Henry Charles Lea, *A History of the Inquisition of the Middle Ages*, 3 vols. (New York, 1922), who mentions the branding in the face of some heretics at Palencia in 1236, 2:182. A band of Albigensians who came to England in A.D. 1160 were seized and brought before the Council of Oxford in 1166, and having refused to abjure, were convicted. They were branded on the forehead, their clothes cut to the waist, and then were driven out to die of the cold; see William of Newburgh, *The First Four Books of the "Historia Rerum Anglicarum" (Chronicles of the Reigns of Stephen, Henry II, and Richard I)*, ed. Richard Howlett, 4 vols. (London, 1884), 1:131–134.

7. See for example, Sir James Fitzjames Stephen, *A History of the Criminal Law of England*, 3 vols., 1st ed. 1883 (New York, n.d.), 3:271, where we are informed that (A.D. 1547), "If the vagabond misrepresents the place of his birth he is to be branded in the face, and remain a slave for life."

8. See *Encyclopedia Britannica*, 1966 ed., under *Branding*.

9. Ibid.

10. In Sicily (1221), Frederick II set branding (or confiscation of property) as the punishment for Jews not wearing the Jewish badge; see Raphael Straus, *Die Juden im Königreich Sizilien unter Normannen und Staufern* (Heidelberg, 1910), pp. 104–105. Christian "Judaizers" in early seventeenth-century England were branded on the forehead with the letter "J" as punishment, as for example John Traske of Somerset; see Henry E. I. Phillips, "An Early Stuart Judaising Sect," *The Jewish Historical Society of England (Transactions)*, 15 (1939–45), 66, and though Traske recanted, he wore his stigma—the "J" on his forehead—the rest of his life (p. 68).

11. See Stade, "Das Kainszeichen," pp. 251–252; and see Dölger, *Sphragis,* pp. 23–33.

12. The humiliation associated with that brutality was recently testified to in a newspaper story that reported interviews with several who survived: Marton Stark said that he had his removed in 1951 and now had a scar, but Ericka Jacoby still had hers and said that she did not want it removed—Los Angeles Times, March 23, 1978.

13. *Encyclopedia Britannica,* under *Branding.*

14. Ibid.

15. Ibid., and see Raphael Semmes, *Crime and Punishment in Early Maryland* (Baltimore, 1938) p. 35, who points out that as of 1674 it was required that: "All county justices, however, must provide irons for burning 'malefactors.' One iron was to be marked with the letter 'H,' probably for hog stealers, and another with the letter 'R,' possibly for runaway servants." In addition sheriffs were to provide two irons, one with the letter "M" and the other with "T," probably to be used for branding murderers and thieves. See also p. 69 where another provision for branding hog stealers with the letter "H" on the shoulder with a red-hot iron is described.

16. As pointed out by W. D. Hambly in an excellent history of body marking covering all periods, places, and cultures: *The History of Tattooing and Its Significance* (New York, 1927), p. 76. See especially the section on "Religious Sanction for Tattooing," pp. 74–80, and "Body Marking with Animal Designs," which in many instances are of a totemic and religious nature, pp. 86–93.

17. See *Encyclopedia Judaica* under *Tefillin* for a good summary of their use and history, and see Alfred Rubens, *A History of Jewish Costume,* 2d ed. (London, 1967 and 1973), pp. 5, 8, 11, 17, 23, 80, and especially fig. 12, p. 9. See also Elizabeth Revel-Neher, "Problèmes d'Iconographie

Judéo-Chrétienne: Le Thème de la Coiffure du Cohen Gadol dans l'Art Byzantin," *Journal of Jewish Art,* 1 (1974), 50–65.

18. See Joshua Trachtenberg, *Jewish Magic and Superstition*, 1st ed. 1939 (Cleveland, New York, and Philadelphia, reprint of 1961), pp. 145–146. The Hebrew letter *Shin* which stands for *Shaddai*—one of the names of the Lord—is embossed on the leather boxes of the tefillin; I am indebted to Bezalel Narkiss for this information.

19. See above, p. 7.

20. Bowker, *The Targums and Rabbinic Literature*, p. 133 (verse 15).

21. Trachtenberg, *Jewish Magic and Superstition*, p. 91, says for example: "First among the names, both in time and in occult power, was the four-letter YHVH, the original name of God. Its powers were ascribed also to a wide range of variations upon it, from the particles YAH, YAHU, HU, etc., to the twelve forms which it could assume by the transposition of its letters . . ."

22. Vermes, "The Targumic Versions of Gen. IV 3–16," p. 105.

23. *Pirkê de Rabbi Eliezer,* p. 156. The editor says in note 4: "The first editions add: 'which are in the Torah and wrote (it).'"

24. *The Zohar,* Zohar I, 36b, vol. 1, p. 137.

25. And, according to Louis Ginzberg, *Sefer ha-Tagin* in *Yalhut Reubeni* says that Cain received the letter "nine" on his arm as a sign that he would not die before he has begotten nine descendants, *Legends of the Jews,* 5:141.

26. *The Pentateuch and Rashi's Commentary,* trans. Abraham Ben Isaiah and Benjamin Sharfman (Brooklyn, 1949), 1:41; and see *Pentateuch with Targum Onkelos, Haphtaroth and Rashi's Commentary,* trans. and ed. M. Rosenbaum and A. M. Silbermann (New York, n.d.), 1:19 where the following is observed: "Other editions of Rashi add the fol-

lowing: another interpretation of 'Whoever will find me will slay me:' this refers to cattle and beasts, since there were then no human beings . . . God immediately set a sign for Cain, viz., he again made the animals be in fear of him."

27. *The Pentateuch and Rashi's Commentary*, p. 43 and 45.

28. I am indebted to Jonas Greenfield for bringing this to my attention; see Sebastian P. Brock, "A Syriac *Life of Abel*," *Le Muséon*, 87(1974), 467–492.

29. Ibid., pp. 467–468.

30. Ibid., p. 478.

31. Ibid., p. 481.

32. Stanislav Segert pointed out some equivalents (to me in a letter of Dec. 26, 1977) from *A Compendious Syriac Dictionary*, ed. J. Payne Smith (Oxford, 1903), of "Fearful, formidable, dreadful, awful." Yet, with no additional details offered by Symmachus, and with an insufficient context, a conclusive decision about the meaning of "terrible sign on his forehead" is impossible.

33. *Life of Abel*, p. 482.

34. Ibid. pp. 483–484.

35. Fr. Klaeber, *Beowulf and the Fight at Finnsburg*, 3d ed. (Lexington, Mass., 1950).

36. See G. P. Krapp, ed., *The Junius Manuscript, The Anglo-Saxon Poetic Records*, Vol. I (New York and London, 1931), lines 1040–1047, p. 34.

37. *Cursor Mundi (The Cursor o the World)* ed. Richard Morris, Early English Text Society (London, 1874–1892), 1:76–77 (lines 1177–1182).

38. *Le Mystère de la Passion d'Arnoul Gréban*, ed. Omer Jodogne, in *Memoires*, classe des lettres, 2d ser., XII (Bruxelles: Académie Royale de Belgique, 1965). This play was composed in the middle of the fifteenth century; for details about it and the author, see Grace Frank, *The Medieval French Drama*, 1st ed. 1954 (Oxford, reprint with corrections, 1972), pp. 181–187.

39. *Mystère de la Passion*, p. 24, lines 980–983.

40. See Grace Frank, *The Medieval French Drama*, pp. 182–183.

41. Ibid., p. 184.

42. Ibid., p. 181.

43. Ibid., p. 182.

44. Ibid., p. 183.

45. Ibid.

46. Lucy Toulmin Smith, ed., *York Plays: The Plays Performed by the Crafts or Mysteries of York on the Day of Corpus Christi in the 14th, 15th, and 16th Centuries* (Oxford, 1885), p. 39, lines 127–135.

47. V. A. Kolve, *The Play called Corpus Christi* (Stanford, Calif., 1966), p. 1.

48. Truman Guy Steffan, *Lord Byron's Cain* (Austin, Texas and London, 1968). For the text quoted in this study, see pp. 254–255, lines 492–502.

49. In Canto I, stanza 83 of *Childe Harold* (the poem appeared about 1812):

And Vice, that digs her own voluptuous tomb,
Had buried long his hopes, no more to rise:
Pleasure's pall'd victim! life-abhorring gloom
Wrote on his faded brow curst Cain's unresting doom.

And in *The Giaour* (published in 1813), at about line 1058:

She died—I dare not tell thee how;
But look—'tis written on my brow!
There read of Cain the curse and crime,
In characters unworn by time:

50. For bibliography on this manuscript, see Otto Pächt and J. J. G. Alexander, *Illuminated Manuscripts in the Bodleian Library* (Oxford, 1973), 3:60, no. 665.

51. Many studies of this iconographic innovation have been written, for example: John Kester Bonnell, "Cain's Jaw Bone," *Publications of the Modern Language Association*, 39 (1924), 140–146; Meyer Schapiro, "Cain's Jaw-Bone

that did the First Murder," *Art Bulletin*, 24 (1942), 205–212; George Henderson, "Cain's Jaw-Bone," *Journal of the Warburg and Courtauld Institutes*, 24 (1961), 108–114; A. A. Barb, "Cain's Murder-Weapon, and Samson's Jawbone of an Ass," *Journal of the Warburg and Courtauld Institutes*, 35 (1972), 386–389.

52. See Fehr, *Das Recht im Bilde*, 1:106.

53. For photos and descriptions published before the fire, see Roberto Papini, *Catalogo delle cose d'arte e di antichità d'Italia*, Ministero della educazione nazionale. Serie I, Fasc. II, parte II (Rome, 1932), pp. 225 ff. and plates XXIII–XXVI.

54. For a fascinating and full study of this legend, see George K. Anderson, *The Legend of the Wandering Jew* (Providence: Brown University Press, 1965). And also see the chapter about Cain and Ahasuerus by Peter L. Thorslev, Jr., *The Byronic Hero* (Minneapolis, 1962), pp. 92–107.

55. Anderson, *Legend of the Wandering Jew*, p. 179.

56. Ibid.

57. Ibid., pp. 178–179.

58. Ibid. A cross on the Wandering Jew's forehead would tie together the idea of the mark of Cain and alleged culpability of the Jews.

59. Ibid.

60. Ibid.

61. This dictionary was translated into English and published at least as early as 1734; see Pierre Bayle, *The Dictionary Historical and Critical of Mr. Peter Bayle,* 2d ed., 5 vols. (London: J. J. & P. Knapton, etc., 1734–1738); in vol. 2 under *Cain,* p. 247, Bayle lists one of the interpretations given for the mark of Cain as: "It was the Sign of the Cross," and his footnote refers readers to Saldenus (a Protestant Dutch theologian of the seventeenth century). Another edition appeared about the same time (1st ed.?) under a different title, *A General Dictionary, Historical and*

Critical . . . , 10 vols. (London: G. Strahan, etc., 1734–1741).

62. Anderson, *Legend of the Wandering Jew*, p. 179, states: "Whether this detail is due to the currency of Lewis' novel, which was long popular, or to an already established folkloristic tradition, must remain unanswered; I prefer the former explanation, but it is well to remember that it has not been mentioned in any of the folk tales cited thus far in the development of the Legend. In brief, since *The Monk* was read by many thousands, I am inclined to raise his importance over that of Xeniola, whoever he was."

63. This apparently has no basis in Jewish legend or exegesis, but arises from the Septuagint translation of נע ונד as στένων καὶ τρέμων, first translated as "gemens et tremens," and only later in Jerome's Vulgate brought closer to the Hebrew as "vagus et profugus."

64. This translation is from *Saint Ambrose, Hexameron, Paradise, and Cain and Abel,* p. 432. The Latin reads: "nam quomodo absoluitur purae illic caelestique sententiae quem nec terrae potuerunt absoluere? et ideo gemens et tremens iubetur esse super terram"; see *De Cain et Abel (CSEL),* p. 404, section 31.

65. Basil, Letter 260, pp. 61–62.

66. Basil, Letter 260, p. 62.

67. Sancti Aureli Augustini, *Contra Faustum,* libri XXXIII, *CSEL,* 25, sect. 6, pt. 1, (Prague, Vienna, Leipzig, 1891), pp. 337–344. For an English translation, see *The Works of Aurelius Augustine, Bishop of Hippo: A New Translation,* ed. Marcus Dods, *Library of the Fathers* (Edinburgh, 1872), vol. 5, "Reply to Faustus the Manichaean," Book XII, pp. 209–214.

68. Jerome, *Ad Damasum,* Letter no. 36, section 2, p. 53. The Latin (on a parallel page) reads: "'Eicior,' inquit, 'a conspectu tuo, et conscientia sceleris lucem ipsam ferre non sustinens abscondar ut latitem, eritque: omnis qui inuenerit

me occidet me, dum ex tremore corporis et furiatae mentis agitatu eum esse intellegit qui mereatur interfici.'"

69. *Commentarii in Genesin, Patrologia Greco-Latina,* vol. 87, col. 249.

70. Ibid., cols. 249–252.

71. Abraham Levene, *The Early Syrian Fathers on Genesis* (London, 1951), pp. 166–167 (commentary of folio 5b line 23). This manuscript on the Pentateuch is from the Mingana Collection; the editor (Levene), p. vii, comments thus about its contents: "It comprised the notes and comments, the views and opinions, and the elucidations and expositions of the early Syrian teachers and their scholars chiefly Nestorian, and most probably emanating from the ancient seminary of Nisibis."

72. See above, p. 30.

73. *Life of Abel,* p. 481.

74. See above, p. 31.

75. *Life of Abel,* p. 483.

76. See *The Book of Adam and Eve, also called The Conflict of Adam and Eve with Satan,* ed. S. C. Malan (London, 1882). The editor (p. v) said: "It is probably the work of some pious and orthodox Egyptian of the fifth or sixth century, who tells his story, or stories—some of which are also found in the Talmud and thence in the Coran and elsewhere—as they were then believed." He further pointed out (p. vi) that the Ethiopic version appears to have been a translation of an Arabic original, and may also date "from the fifth or sixth century."

77. *Book of Adam and Eve,* p. 103.

78. Ibid.

79. Ibid.

80. Ibid.

81. Ibid.

82. Bede, *In Genesim,* ed. Ch. W. Jones, *Corpus Christianorum,* vol. 118A (Turnhout, 1967), p. 80: "Ipsum

uidelicet signum quod *tremens et gemens uagusque et profugus* semper uiueret, eadem sua aerumna admonitus quia non passim a quibuslibet posset occidi. Quicumque autem eum occideret, uel magnis miseriis ipsum Cain liberaret uel se ipsum hoc faciens septemplici uindictae manciparet."

83. *Opuscula exegetica: Interrogationes et responsiones in Genesin*, inter. 89, *Pat. Lat.*, vol. 100, col. 525.

84. *Commentarius in Genesim, Pat. Lat.*, vol. 111, col. 507.

85. *Commentarius in Genesim, Pat. Lat.*, vol. 115, col. 151.

86. As for example, Rabanus Maurus (see above, note 84): "ipsum videlicet signum, quod tremens et gemens, vagus et profugus semper viveret, nec audere eum uspiam orbis terrarum sedes habere quietas; et forte idcirco civitatem condidit in qua salvari posset."

87. *Commentarius in Genesim, Pat. Lat.*, vol. 131, col. 70: "Hoc videlicet, quia vagus et profugus erat super terram, vel, ut LXX, gemens et contremens."

88. *Expositio in Genesim, Pat. Lat.*, vol. 164, col. 174: "Hoc autem signum membrorum tremor fuisse dicitur, quia quasi insaniens, et melancholico similis, ad miseriam sui homines provocabat. Quis enim occidere vellet, qui ipsa morte deteriora pati videbatur."

89. *Adnotationes et Elucidatoriae in Pentateuchon. Pat. Lat.*, vol. 175, col. 44, "id est tremorem membrorum quasi fanatici, id est furibundi (spastici, i.e., concussi et stare nequeuntis), unde dignus apparebat misericordia, quia percussus erat ira Dei, et excommunicatus."

90. See Beryl Smalley, *The Study of the Bible in the Middle Ages*, 1st ed. 1940 (Oxford, 2d ed., 1952), pp. 178–179.

91. *Historia Scholastica, Liber Genesis, Pat. Lat.*, vol. 198, col. 1078, "Et posuit Deus signum in Cain, tremorem capitis. Quia fratrem suum, qui erat caput Ecclesiae oc-

ciderat, ut sic sciretur a Domino punitus excommunicatus, et indignus misericordia, nec interficeretur."

92. "Dat ergo Cain signum cito ne perimatur, / Et motus capitis et tremor illud erat." See Paul E. Beichner, ed., *Aurora Petri Rigae Biblia Versificata: A Verse Commentary on the Bible*. Pt. I (Notre Dame, 1965), p. 43, lines 417–418.

93. Ibid., p. xi.

94. This letter has been published—both the Latin and an English translation—by Solomon Grayzel, *The Church and the Jews in the XIIIth Century*, 1st ed. 1933 (New York, rev. ed., 1966), pp. 126–127.

95. Carl Horstmann, ed., *Sammlung Altenglischer Legenden* (Heilbronn, 1878), p. 224, lines 43–45.

96. *De Sancta Trinitate et Operibus Eius,* ed. Hrabanus Haacke, *Corpus Christianorum,* 21 (Turnhout, 1971), 293.

97. Ibid., "sed *posuit,* inquit, *Cain in signum,* id est, quasi signum, uidelicet, ut sic non auderet aliquis pro ultione contingere illum, quomodo nemo debet amouere regis uel imperatoris signum. De quo placito suo quis reprehendere posset legis auctorem ante datam legem, cum sub lege uiuens homo licet rex paene fecerit idem? . . . Illud simile est huic. Hoc modo rex in signum posuit illum qui occiderat reum habiturus eum quicumque ex cognatis ulcisceretur sanguinem occisi, ueluti qui regii signum temerasset edicti, sapienter utique; quia ex huiusmodi ultione multiplicantur proximi sanguinis et proinde nemo iure reprehendit. Quanto magis, cum per semetipsum Deus hoc agit, sapientiae debet ascribi et reus habendus erat, qui huiusmodi edictum eius temerauit?"

98. To be discussed later in this study.

99. Rupert, *De Sancta Trinitate et Operibus Eius,* p. 293 (quoted at n. 173 below).

100. Guido Kisch, *Pseudo-Philo's Liber Antiquarum Biblicarum* (Notre Dame, 1949), p. 113 for the Latin. An En-

glish translation is published in Bowker, *The Targums and Rabbinic Literature*, Appendix I, pp. 301–314. See also Daniel J. Harrington, *The Hebrew Fragments of Pseudo-Philo* (Missoula, 1974).

101. Bowker, *The Targums*, p. 301.

102. *The Pentateuch and Rashi's Commentary*, p. 42.

103. See my comments about this subject in, "Cain's monstrous progeny in *Beowulf*: Part I, Noachic tradition," *Anglo-Saxon England*, 8 (1979), p. 153.

104. *Liber Hebraicarum Quaestionum in Genesim, Pat. Lat.,* vol. 23, col. 994, where Jerome says, "Non est igitur terra *Naid*, ut vulgus nostrorum putat; sed expletur sententia Dei, quod huc atque illuc vagus et profugus oberravit."

105. James de Rothschild, ed., *Le Mistère du viel Testament*, 6 vols. (Paris, 1878–1891), vol. 1. This play is a late one, yet it contains almost entirely medieval traditions. Grace Frank, *Medieval French Drama*, p. 194, says that references in the fifteenth and sixteenth centuries to performances of the *Vieux Testament* "probably allude to performances of individual plays rather than of the whole vast disparate compilation which survives."

106. Frank, *Medieval French Drama*, p. 196, pointed this out.

107. The French quotations are all from the Rothschild edition cited above in n. 105.

108. Dionysius the Carthusian [Denys van Leeuwen], *Opera omnia in unum corpus digesta ad fidem . . .* , 42 vols. in 44 (Monstrolii, 1896–1935), 1:131, section C: "quod signum seu plaga, fuit (ut aliqui dicunt) vehemens capitis tremor. Alii dicunt, quod fuit horribilis tremor omnium membrorum ipsius, et cum hoc impressio quaedam in vultu ejus."

109. Cornelius à Lapide [Cornelius van den Steen], *Commentaria in Scripturam Sacram* (Paris, 1868–1880), 1:120, "Verum communior sententia est, signum hoc fuisse tre-

morem corporis, et mentis ac vultus consternationem, ita ut corpus et vultus peccatum Caini loquerentur. Hunc enim tremorem fuisse in Caino, patet ex Septuaginta."

110. Bayle, *The Dictionary Historical and Critical,* vol. 2, under *Cain.*

111. Bayle mentions it among his list of interpretations, ibid. Ginzberg, *Legends of the Jews,* 5:141, n. 48, suggested that "leprosy was inflicted as a punishment upon those who devoted their lives to the acquisition of possessions."

112. *Lebor Gabála Érenn,* ed. R. A. Stewart Macalister, Irish Texts Society, 34(1938), Part I, p. 87.

113. See *The Medieval Literature of Western Europe,* general ed., John H. Fisher (New York, 1966), chap. XI, "Medieval Celtic Literature," by Charles Donahue, pp. 395–396.

114. Donahue, "Medieval Celtic Literature," p. 396 and *Lebor Gabála Érenn,* ed. Macalister, pp. xxv–xxxiii.

115. Macalister, ibid.

116. Francis Wormald, *The Winchester Psalter* (London, 1973), folio 20 (fig. 23), and folio 21 (fig. 24).

117. *Lebor Gabála,* p. 181.

118. *Legends of the Jews,* 5:141, n. 28, part 4.

119. See my brief summary of this subject, *The Horned Moses in Medieval Art and Thought* (Berkeley, Los Angeles, London, 1970), pp. 1–5.

120. Ibid., chapter on the "Ambiguity of the Meaning of Horns," pp. 121–140.

121. For a summary of these legends along with references, see Vigdor Aptowitzer, *Kain und Abel in der Agada* . . (Vienna and Leipzig, 1922), pp. 56–82.

122. Probably first appeared in the Book of Jubilees: "At the close of this jubilee Cain was killed after him in the same year; for his house fell upon him and he died in the midst of his house, and he was killed by its stones; for with a stone he had killed Abel, and by a stone was he killed in

righteous judgment." Quoted from R. H. Charles, *The Apocrypha and Pseudepigrapha* (Oxford, 1913; reprint of 1973), vol. II, *Pseudepigrapha,* p. 19, lines 31–33.

123. A separate and more complete study of this theme still needs to be done, but a fair amount has been collected and published, for example, by Edmund Reiss, "The story of Lamech and its place in medieval drama," *Journal of Medieval and Renaissance Studies* 2 (1972), 35–48; see also Raphael Loewe, "The Mediaeval Christian Hebraists of England," *Hebrew Union College Annual,* 28 (1957), 205–252. I am indebted to Malachi Beit-Arié who brought this last reference to my attention.

124. In the Greek Octateuchs of the eleventh and twelfth centuries.

125. In one of the eleventh-century Catalan Bibles, Paris, Bibl. Natl. lat. 6[I], known as the Roda Bible, folio 6 recto.

126. As part of the sculptured Genesis scenes on the facade of the cathedral at Modena, Italy.

127. For a description of the development of the Tanhuma Midrash, see Bowker, *The Targums,* pp. 76–77. It is, of course, a compilation, but its final redaction is possibly ninth century; see Martin McNamara, *The New Testament and the Palestinian Targum to the Pentateuch* (Rome, 1966), p. 91.

128. From *Midrash Tanhuma* (New York–Berlin, reprint of 1927), Genesis, sections 10 and 11 (leaf 12B), p. 24.

129. The Jewish origin of this motif was noted by Francis Salet, *La Madeleine de Vézelay* (Melun, 1948), p. 184, no. 22.

130. Burgundy of the twelfth century is the setting for more bizarre Jewish folklore. Ancient legend described a strange story of a hairy-legged Queen of Sheba (Eastern), or, as transposed in the West, a goose-footed (or web-footed) Queen. Though the documented life of the latter

seems to have been restricted to medieval Germany, it is only in French churches of the twelfth century that the goose-footed queen appeared. See James B. Pritchard, *Solomon and Sheba* (London, 1974), pp. 137 ff.

131. Jacques Issaverdens, *The Uncanonical Writings of the Old Testament* (Venice, 1901), p. 10.

132. Gerard Brault pointed out to me that there are other examples of "singing bone" themes, as for example the one recorded in the Thompson Motif Index, vol. 2, Motif E 632. And I am indebted to Michael Stone who pointed out that one of the horns in Daniel 7:8 speaks— "and behold eyes like the eyes of a man were in this horn, and a mouth speaking great things."

133. Issaverdens, *Uncanonical Writings*, p. 59.

134. Ibid.

135. Ibid.

136. Ibid., p. 75.

137. Ibid.

138. Ibid., p. 60, "And God brought from above a skin and covered him."

139. Ibid.

140. For a superb discussion of this manuscript and a facsimile of all the folios, see *The Holkham Bible Picture Book*, introd. and commentary by W. O. Hassall (London, 1954). The Anglo-Norman text has been edited by F. P. Pickering, *The Anglo-Norman Text of the Holkham Bible Picture Book*, Anglo-Norman Text Society, XXIII (Oxford, 1971).

141. Hassall, *Holkham Bible Picture Book*, p. 69.

142. See above, n. 123.

143. See above, pp. 57–59.

144. *Lebor Gabála,* p. 183.

145. Ibid., p. 87.

146. Edited by Whitley Stokes, *Transactions of the Philo-*

logical Society (1864), pp. 1–208. At the time of this edition there were still four copies in existence. The Stokes edition was based on the oldest—dated August 12, 1611.

147. Ibid., p. 4; and see *The Cornish Ordinalia,* trans. Markham Harris (Washington, D.C., 1969), p. xii.

148. E. Bernard, "La Création du Monde, mystère Breton," *Revue Celtique,* 9 (1888), 152–153.

149. *Creation of the World,* Stokes ed., p. 4; and see E. K. Chambers, *The Mediaeval Stage,* 1st ed. 1903 (London, repr. 1967), II:435.

150. K. S. Block, *Ludus Coventriae or the Plaie Called Corpus Christi,* Early English Text Society, e.s. 120 (London, 1922), p. 40, line 166: "Vndyr ʒon grett busche mayster. A best do I see [Under yon great bush, Master, a beast do I see.]"

151. *Creation of the World,* pp. 94–95, lines 1181–1183.

152. Ibid., p. 95, following line 1181. Stage instructions in this edition only appear interspersed in the Cornish version on parallel pages with the English translation.

153. Ibid., pp. 108–109, lines 1371–1378.

154. Ibid., pp. 110–111, lines 1379–1381.

155. Ibid., pp. 118–119, lines 1498–1506.

156. Ibid., lines 1507–1521.

157. Ibid., pp. 124–125, lines 1589–1590.

158. Ibid., lines 1593–1595.

159. Ibid., pp. 126–127, lines 1616–1620.

160. Ibid., pp. 128–129, lines 1624–1625.

161. Ibid., lines 1643–1644.

162. See above, p. 65.

163. Harburg Oettingen-Wallerstein Collection, MS. 1, 2, lat. 4°, 15. See the study of the Pamplona Bibles by François Bucher, *The Pamplona Bibles,* 2 vols. (New Haven and London, 1970).

164. Reproduced by Bucher, vol. 2, plate 13.

165. I am indebted to Georgia Ronan Crampton for calling this woodcut to my attention.

166. See for example, Mellinkoff, *The Horned Moses in Medieval Art and Thought*, p. 66, where I noted that "the logical biblical sequence for giving horns to Moses was not always observed. Moses was often pictured with horns in events that took place before Exodus 34:29."

167. In fact, the legend that Lamech killed Cain is denied in the Genesis Rabbah; see the translation edition, *Midrash Rabbah*, vol. 1, Bereshith XXIII. 4, p. 195, where Lamech says: "Cain slew, yet judgment was suspended for him for seven generations; for me, who did not slay, surely judgment will wait seventy-seven generations!"

168. See above, p. 67.

169. This has recently been completely translated; see *The Irish Adam and Eve Story from Saltair Na Rann*, 2 vols., volume 1: text and translation by David Greene and Fergus Kelly; vol. 2: commentary by Brian O. Murdoch (Dublin Institute for Advanced Studies, 1976).

170. Brian Murdoch, "An Early Irish Adam and Eve: *Saltair na Rann* and the Traditions of the Fall," *Mediaeval Studies*, 35 (1973), 147, where Murdoch says that it was written between 985 and 990.

171. *The Irish Adam and Eve*, 1:93.

172. Ibid.

173. Rupert of Deutz, *De Sancta Trinitate*, p. 293: "Et posuit Dominus signum in Cain, ut uerbi gratia, tremulo corpore uiueret uel cornu in fronte gestaret uel tale quid, quod non ex auctoritate Scripturae sed ex iudaicis fabulis est."

174. See Avrom Saltman, *Pseudo-Jerome, Quaestiones on the Book of Samuel* (Leiden, 1975), p. 34: "Rupert's interest in the *Quaestiones Hebraicae* may have led him to take an active part in the Christian-Jewish polemic of the period.

Shortly before his death in 1129 he succeeded in undermining the Jewish faith of Judah ben David Ha-Levi of Cologne. Under his Christian name Hermannus, Judah subsequently enjoyed a fairly distinguished career in the Premonstratensian Order." See also, *Hermannus quondam Judaeus opusculum de conversione sua,* ed. G. Niemeyer [Monumenta Germaniae Historica: Quellen zur Geistesgeschichte des Mittelalters iv], (Weimar, 1963), pp. 76 ff., concerning Rupert's interest in the Christian-Jewish polemic of the period.

175. Cambridge, St. Johns College Library MS. K. 26.

176. As aptly stated by Louis Ginzberg, *Legends of the Jews,* 5: viii, "One of the outstanding characteristics of 'the popular mind' is its conservatism and adherence to old forms." And as M. René Guénon said: "The very conception of 'folklore,' as commonly understood, rests on a fundamentally false hypothesis, the supposition, viz., that there really are such things as 'popular creation' or spontaneous inventions of the masses; and the connection of this point of view with the democratic prejudice is obvious . . . The folk has thus preserved, without understanding, the remains of old traditions that go back sometimes to an indeterminably distant past." This is quoted by Ananda K. Coomaraswamy, "The Nature of 'Folklore' and 'Popular Art,'" *Indian Art and Letters,* 11, 2 (1937), 81.

177. As written to me in a letter of February 27, 1978 from Professor Haijo Jan Westra.

178. See the comments on this by E. H. Gombrich, "Bosch's 'Garden of Earthly Delights': A Progress Report," *Journal of the Warburg and Courtauld Institutes,* 32 (1969), 165; and see G. K. Hunter, "Othello and Colour Prejudice," *Proceedings of the British Academy,* 53 (1967), 147–148.

179. Though the belief had little theological sanction (since Cain's descendants were all supposed to have per-

ished in the flood), yet there was ample confusion about that issue and about the actual descendants of Cain. See my forthcoming study, "Cain's monstrous progeny in *Beowulf*: Part II, post-diluvian survival," *Anglo-Saxon England,* 9 (1980). A pre-Adamite theory was, moreover, developed in the mid-seventeenth century by Isaac de la Peyrère who argued that the Negroes belong to a pre-Adamite race related to Cain. See D. R. McKee, "Isaac de la Peyrère, a Precursor of Eighteenth-Century Critical Deists," *PMLA* 59 (1944), 456–485 and Thomas F. Gossett, *Race, The History of an Idea in America* (Dallas, 1963), p. 15.

180. But for some good examples see, Hunter, "Othello and Colour Prejudice," pp. 142–144. And see *The Image of the Black in Western Art,* gen. ed. Ladislas Bugner, vol. 1 (New York, 1976), vol. 2 in 2 parts (New York, 1979).

181. *Midrash Rabbah,* vol. 1, Bereshith XXII. 6, p. 184, and the editor, note 4, stated: "*Wayyihar* is derived from *harah,* to burn."

182. Ibid. Louis Ginzberg also translated this as blackened, *Legends of the Jews,* 1:108: "Besides a chastisement was inflicted upon him. His face turned black as smoke." Also see 5:137, n. 13, where Ginzberg says: "The blackening of the face is perhaps to be taken as a contrast to its original heavenly splendor." That this was the traditional way to interpret the Hebrew seems to be the case; it was in fact picked up by S. Baring-Gould, *Legends of the Patriarchs and Prophets* (New York, 1872), who said, (without giving his source), p. 74: "With regard to the mark put upon Cain, there is diverging of opinion. Some say that his tongue turned white; others, that he was given a peculiar dress; others, that his face became black . . . ."

183. Issaverdens, *Uncanonical Writings,* pp. 54–55.

184. See Mellinkoff, "Cain's monstrous progeny in *Beowulf:* Part II, post-diluvian survival," *Anglo-Saxon England,* 9 (1980), in press.

185. As translated by Oliver F. Emerson, "Legends of Cain, Especially in Old and Middle English," *Publications of the Modern Language Association,* 21 (1906), 884. He used the text edited by Joseph Diemer, *Genesis und Exodus nach der Millstätter Handschrift* (Vienna, 1862) where the German reads, p. 26: "Sumelich uluren begarwe [ir uil] schone uarwe, si werden swarz und eislich, [dem] do niht was gelich." It also appears in the Vienna manuscript; see Viktor Dollmayr, *Die altdeutsche Genesis nach der Wiener Handschrift* (Halle [Saale], 1932), p. 37, lines 1306–1309.

186. See Mellinkoff, "Cain's monstrous progeny in *Beowulf:* Part II, post-diluvian survival," in press.

187. This is one of the major Mormon tracts. Any edition published by the Church of Jesus Christ of Latter-day Saints, Salt Lake City, Utah, can be used to follow or check the quotations used in this study. The first edition was published in 1851 by Franklin D. Richards. For a history of its publication and for an interesting study of Mormonism, see the Master's Thesis by Naomi Felicia Woodbury, *A Legacy of Intolerance: Nineteenth Century Pro-Slavery Propaganda and the Mormon Church Today*, University of California at Los Angeles, 1966. I am indebted to Ann Hinckley for bringing this to my attention. (It is interesting to note, by the way, that a version of the Lamech legend is also included among these revelations. There is obviously a need for a scholarly tracing of these and other ancient legends revived by J. Smith in his theological writings.)

188. *The Book of Moses* forms the first part of the *Pearl of Great Price* and contains 8 chapters.

189. *The Book of Abraham* follows the *Book of Moses* and contains 5 chapters.

190. *Mormon Doctrine* (Salt Lake City, Utah, 1966).

191. *Mormonism and the Negro* (Orem, Utah, 1960).

192. *The Church and the Negro* (n.p., 1967).

193. Ibid., pp. 12–14.

194. Ibid., p. 13.

195. Ibid., pp. 14–17.

196. As, for example, reported on the front page of The New York Times, June 10, 1978, by Kenneth A. Briggs, "The 148-year-old policy of excluding black men from the Mormon priesthood was struck down by the church's leaders yesterday."

4. INTENTIONALLY DISTORTED INTERPRETATIONS

1. For an edition and history of the play, see A. C. Cawley, ed., *The Wakefield Pageants in the Towneley Cycle* (Manchester, 1958).

2. Ibid., p. xi.

3. Ibid., pp. xx–xxi.

4. Edith Harnett, "Cain in the Medieval *Towneley* Play," *Annuale Mediaevale*, 12 (1971), 24.

5. "The Law of Man and the Peace of God: Judicial Process as Satiric Theme in the Wakefield *Mactacio Abel*," *Speculum*, 49 (1974), 699–707.

6. Ibid., p. 702.

7. Cawley, *Wakefield Pageants*, p. 10, lines 370–373.

8. Ibid., p. 11, lines 402–405.

9. Ibid., p. 11, lines 406–409.

10. Brockman, "The Law of Man," p. 700.

11. Cawley, p. 94, n. 408.

12. Brockman, "The Law of Man," pp. 701–703.

13. Cawley, *Wakefield Pageants*, p. 12, lines 419–435.

14. Ibid., lines 445–448.

15. Brockman, "The Law of Man," p. 701.

16. Ibid., p. 702.

17. Ibid.

18. Ibid., pp. 706–707.

19. I am indebted to Robert Benson who brought this charming tale to my attention. It appears in letter 116; see *Opus Epistolarum Des. Erasmi Roterdami,* ed. P. S. Allen (Oxford, 1906), 1:268–271. The letter has been interestingly analyzed by Roland H. Bainton, "Man, God, and the Church in the Age of the Renaissance," *The Renaissance, Six Essays* (New York, 1953) pp. 82–83.

20. Hermann Hesse, *Demian,* Bantam paperback edition (New York, 1970), pp. 24–25.

21. Ibid., p. 25.

22. Ibid., p. 107.

23. Ibid., p. 114.

24. Ibid.

25. Ibid.

26. Ibid.

27. Ibid., p. 122.

28. Ibid., pp. 114–115.

5. CAIN'S MARK AND THE JEWS

1. *De Cain et Abel, CSEL.*

2. *Cain and Abel,* trans. John Savage, p. 362. The Latin, *CSEL,* p. 341, reads: "haec figura synagogae et ecclesiae in istis duobus fratribus ante praecessit, Cain et Abel. per Cain parricidalis populus intellegitur Iudaeorum, qui domini et auctoris sui et secundum Mariae uirginis partum fratris, ut ita dicam, sanguinem persecutus est, per Abel autem intellegitur Christianus adhaerens deo, . . ."

3. Sancti Aureli Augustini, *Contra Faustum, CSEL,* 25, sect. 6, pt. 1, pp. 337–343.

4. The Latin, *CSEL,* p. 342, reads: "Et posuit dominus deus Cain signum, ne eum occidat omnis, qui inuenerit. hoc reuera multum mirabile est, quemadmodum omnes gentes, quae a Romanis subiugatae sunt, in ritum Romanorum sacrorum transierint eaque sacrilega ob-

seruanda et celebranda susceperint, gens autem Iudaea siue sub paganis regibus siue sub christianis non amiserit signum legis suae, quo a ceteris gentibus populisque distinguitur; et omnis imperator uel rex, qui eos in regno suo inuenit, cum ipso signo eos inuenit nec occidit, id est non efficit, ut non sint Iudaei, certo quodam et proprio suae obseruationis signo a ceterarum gentium communione discreti, nisi quicumque eorum ad Christum transierit, ut iam non inueniatur Cain nec exeat a facie dei nec habitet in terra Naim, id quod dicitur interpretari 'commotio.'"

5. Bede, *In Genesim,* ed. Jones, p. 84.

6. *Quaestiones in Vetus Testamentum, Pat. Lat.,* vol. 83, col. 226.

7. *Commentarius in Genesim, Pat. Lat.,* vol. 107, col. 507.

8. *Commentarius in Genesim, Pat. Lat.,* vol. 131, col. 70.

9. *Expositio in Genesim, Pat. Lat.,* vol. 164, col. 174.

10. *Aurora,* ed. Beichner, p. 44, lines 443–450.

11. *The Letters of Peter the Venerable,* ed. Giles Constable, 2 vols. (Cambridge, Mass., 1967), I:327–330.

12. Grayzel, *The Church and the Jews in the XIIIth Century,* pp. 126–127.

13. Grayzel published the decree in Latin and English, ibid., pp. 308–309.

14. See ibid., for a summary, p. 61, n. 97.

15. Ibid., and see Grayzel's discussion, p 61.

16. Ibid., pp. 61–70. See also Guido Kisch, "The Yellow Badge in History," *Historia Judaica,* 19 (1957), 91–101; and, see Mellinkoff, *The Horned Moses,* pp. 128–130, and references in the notes to those pages.

17. See my article, "The Round-topped Tablets of the Law: Sacred Symbol and Emblem of Evil," *Journal of Jewish Art,* 1 (1974), 40.

18. See Grayzel, *The Church and the Jews,* pp. 69–70, who said: "The decree was forced upon the Jews in the usual manner, by indirect excommunication, or by ex-

hortation and threats to the secular rulers. In this case the princes saw no direct financial loss, but on the contrary a new source of income from fines and monopoly."

19. Ibid., pp. 140–141.

20. Mellinkoff, "Round-topped Tablets of the Law," p. 40.

21. Kisch, "The Yellow Badge," pp. 115–121, and Grayzel, pp. 41–82.

22. Kisch, "The Yellow Badge," pp. 140–141.

23. Ibid., p. 121.

24. Ibid., pp. 121–122.

25. Ibid., pp. 123–131. See also Philip Friedman, "The Jewish Badge and the Yellow Star in the Nazi Era," *Historia Judaica,* 17 (1955), 41–70.

Bibliography

AMBROSE [SAINT]. *Hexameron, Paradise, and Cain and Abel.* Translated by John Savage. Fathers of the Church. Vol. 42. New York, 1961.

――――. *Sancti Ambrosii Opera.* Edited by Carolus Schenkl. *Corpus Scriptorum Ecclesiasticorum Latinorum*, vol. 32/1: *De Cain et Abel.* Vienna, Prague, Leipzig, 1897.

ANDERSON, GEORGE K. *The Legend of the Wandering Jew.* Providence, R.I., 1965.

APTOWITZER, VIGDOR. *Kain und Abel in der Agada* . . . Vienna and Leipzig, 1922.

AUGUSTINE, AURELIUS [SAINT]. *Contra Faustum.* Libri XXXIII. *Corpus Scriptorum Ecclesiasticorum Latinorum.* 25, sect. 6, pt. 1. Prague, Vienna, Leipzig, 1891.

――――. *The Works of Aurelius Augustine, Bishop of Hippo: A New Translation.* Vol. 5. Edited by Marcus Dods. Library of the Fathers. Edinburgh, 1872.

BAINTON, ROLAND H. "Man, God, and the Church in the Age of the Renaissance." In *The Renaissance, Six Essays*, pp. 77–96. New York, 1953.

BARB, A. A. "Cain's Murder-Weapon, and Samson's Jawbone of an Ass," *Journal of the Warburg and Courtauld Institutes* 35 (1972), 386–389.

BARING-GOULD, S. *Legends of the Patriarchs and Prophets.* New York, 1872.

BARNES, HARRY ELMER. *The Story of Punishment.* Boston, 1930.

BASIL [SAINT]. *Collected Letters.* Translated by Roy Joseph

Deferrari. Loeb Classical Library. 4 vols. London and Cambridge, Mass., 1926–1934.

BAYLE, PIERRE. *The Dictionary Historical and Critical of Mr. Peter Bayle.* 5 vols. 2d ed. London, 1734–1738. [Another edition appeared about the same time under a different title, *A General Dictionary, Historical and Critical* . . . 10 vols. London: G. Strahan, etc., 1734–1741.]

BEDE. *In Genesim.* Edited by Ch. W. Jones. *Corpus Christianorum,* vol. 118A. Turnhout, 1967.

BEICHNER, PAUL E., ed. *Aurora Petri Rigae Biblia Versificata: A Verse Commentary on the Bible.* Pt. I. Notre Dame, 1965.

BERNARD, E. "La Création du Monde, mystère Breton," *Revue Celtique* 9 (1888), 149–159.

BLATT, FRANZ. *The Latin Josephus.* Copenhagen, 1957.

BLOCK, K. S. *Ludus Coventriae or the Plaie Called Corpus Christi.* Early English Text Society, e.s. 120. London, 1922.

BONNELL, JOHN KESTER. "Cain's Jaw Bone," *PMLA* 39 (1924), 140–146.

BOWKER, JOHN. *The Targums and Rabbinic Literature.* Cambridge, 1969.

BROCK, SEBASTIAN P. "A Syriac *Life of Abel,*" *Le Muséon* 87 (1974), 467–492.

BROCKMAN, BENNETT. "The Law of Man and the Peace of God: Judicial Process as Satiric Theme in the Wakefield *Mactacio Abel,*" *Speculum* 49 (1974), 699–707.

BUCHER, FRANÇOIS. *The Pamplona Bibles.* 2 vols. New Haven and London, 1970.

CAWLEY, A. C., ed. *The Wakefield Pageants in the Towneley Cycle.* Manchester, 1958.

CHAMBERS, E. K. *The Mediaeval Stage.* 2 vols. London, reprint 1967. [1st ed. 1903]

CHARLES, R. H. *The Apocrypha and Pseudepigrapha,* 2 vols. Oxford, reprint 1973. [1st ed. Oxford, 1913]

A Compendious Syriac Dictionary, edited by J. Payne Smith. Oxford, 1903.

CONSTABLE, GILES, ed. *The Letters of Peter the Venerable*. 2 vols. Cambridge, Mass., 1967.

COOMARASWAMY, ANANDA K. "The Nature of 'Folklore' and 'Popular Art,'" *Indian Art and Letters* 11, 2 (1937), 76–84.

CORNELIUS À LAPIDE [CORNELIUS VAN DEN STEEN]. *Commentaria in Scripturam Sacram*. Paris, 1868–1880.

Cursor Mundi (The Cursor o the World). A Northumbrian poem of the fourteenth century in four versions. Vol. 1. Edited by Richard Morris. Early English Text Society. London, 1874–1892.

DIEMER, Joseph, ed. *Genesis und Exodus nach der Millstätter Handschrift*. 2 vols. Vienna, 1862.

DIONYSIUS THE CARTHUSIAN [Denys van Leeuwen]. *Opera omnia in unum corpus digesta ad fidem* . . . 42 vols. in 44. Monstrolii, 1896–1935.

DOLLMAYR, VIKTOR. *Die altdeutsche Genesis nach der Wiener Handschrift*. Halle [Saale], 1932.

DONAHUE, CHARLES. "Medieval Celtic Literature." In *The Medieval Literature of Western Europe*, edited by John H. Fisher, pp. 381–409. New York, 1966.

EARLE, ALICE MORSE. *Curious Punishments of Bygone Days*. Chicago, 1896.

EISSFELDT, OTTO. *The Old Testament, The History of the Formation of the Old Testament*. Translated by Peter R. Ackroyd. New York, Evanston, San Francisco, London, reprint 1974. [1st ed. 1965, translated from the 3d German edition of 1964; 1st German edition, 1934.]

EMERSON, OLIVER F., trans. "Legends of Cain, Especially in Old and Middle English," *PMLA* 21 (1906), 831–929.

Encyclopedia Judaica. 16 vols. Jerusalem, 1971.

EPSTEIN, ISIDORE, and MAURICE SIMON, ed. and trans. *The Babylonian Talmud*. 18 vols. London, 1961.

ERASMUS, DESIDERIUS. *Opus Epistolarum Des. Erasmi Roterdami*. Edited by P. S. Allen. Oxford, 1906.

FEHR, HANS. *Das Recht im Bilde*. Erlenbach-Zürich, 1923.

FRANK, GRACE. *The Medieval French Drama*. Oxford, reprint 1972. [1st ed. 1954]

FREEDMAN, H., and MAURICE SIMON, ed. and trans. *The Midrash Rabbah*. 10 vols. London, 1939.

FRIEDLANDER, GERALD, trans. *Pirķê de Rabbi Eliezer (The Chapters of Rabbi Eliezer the Great)*. New York, reprint 1970. [1st ed. 1916]

FRIEDMAN, PHILIP. "The Jewish Badge and the Yellow Star in the Nazi Era," *Historia Judaica* 17 (1955), 41–70.

FRYMER-KENSKY, TIKVA. "The Atrahasis Epic and its Significance for our Understanding of Genesis 1–9," *Biblical Archeologist* (Dec., 1977), pp. 147–155.

———. "What the Babylonian Flood Stories can and cannot teach us about the Genesis Flood." *Biblical Archaeology Review* (Nov.–Dec., 1978), pp. 32–41.

GINZBERG, LOUIS. *Legends of the Jews*. 5 vols. Philadelphia, reprint 1947. [1st ed. 1925]

GOMBRICH, E. H. "Bosch's 'Garden of Earthly Delights': A Progress Report," *Journal of the Warburg and Courtauld Institutes* 32 (1969), 162–170.

GOSSETT, THOMAS F. *Race, the History of an Idea in America*. Dallas, 1963.

GRAYZEL, SOLOMON. *The Church and the Jews in the XIIIth Century*. New York, rev. ed. 1966. [1st ed. 1933]

HAMBLY, W. D. *The History of Tattooing and Its Significance*. New York, 1927.

HARNETT, EDITH. "Cain in the Medieval *Towneley* Play," *Annuale Mediaevale* 12 (1971), 21–29.

HARRIS, MARKHAM, trans. *The Cornish Ordinalia*. Washington, D.C., 1969.

HENDERSON, GEORGE. "Cain's Jaw-Bone." *Journal of the Warburg and Courtauld Institutes* 24 (1961), 108–114.

HESSE, HERMANN. *Demian.* New York: Bantam Paperback, 1970.

The Holkham Bible Picture Book. Introduction and commentary by W. O. Hassall. London, 1954.

The Holy Scriptures, According to the Masoretic Text [Hebrew Bible]. Philadelphia, 1917.

HORSTMANN, CARL, ed. *Sammlung Altenglischer Legenden.* Heilbronn, 1878.

HUNTER, G. K. "Othello and Colour Prejudice." *Proceedings of the British Academy* 53 (1967), 139–163.

The Image of the Black in Western Art. Ladislas Bugner, general editor. Vol. 1, New York, 1976. Vol. 2 in 2 parts, New York, 1979.

The Interpreter's Dictionary of the Bible. 4 vols. Nashville, New York, 1962; and supplementary volume, 1976.

The Irish Adam and Eve Story from "Saltair Na Rann." 2 vols. Volume 1: Text and translation by David Greene and Fergus Kelly. Volume 2: Commentary by Brian O. Murdoch. Dublin Institute for Advanced Studies, 1976.

ISSAVERDENS, JACQUES. *The Uncanonical Writings of the Old Testament.* Venice, 1901.

JEROME [SAINT]. *Lettres.* 8 vols. Edited and translated by Jérôme Labourt. Paris, 1949–1963.

JODOGNE, OMER, ed. *Le Mystère de la Passion d'Arnoul Gréban.* In *Memoires,* classe des lettres, 2d ser., XII, Bruxelles, 1965.

JOSEPHUS, FLAVIUS *Jewish Antiquities, Books I–IV.* Translated by H. St. J. Thackeray. London and New York, 1930.

KISCH, GUIDO. *Pseudo-Philo's Liber Antiquarum Biblicarum.* Notre Dame, 1949.

———. "The Yellow Badge in History," *Historia Judaica* 19 (1957), 89–146.

KLAEBER, FR. *Beowulf and the Fight at Finnsburg.* Lexington, Mass., 3d ed. 1950.

KOLVE, V. A. *The Play Called Corpus Christi.* Stanford, Calif., 1966.

KRAPP, G. P., ed. *The Junius Manuscript, The Anglo-Saxon Poetic Records.* Vol. 1. New York and London, 1931.

LEA, HENRY CHARLES. *A History of the Inquisition of the Middle Ages.* 3 vols. New York, 1922.

Lebor Gabála Érenn, The Book of the Taking of Ireland. Edited by R. A. Stewart Macalister. Irish Texts Society, 34 (1938), Part I.

LEVENE, ABRAHAM. *The Early Syrian Fathers on Genesis.* London, 1951.

LOEWE, RAPHAEL. "The Mediaeval Christian Hebraists of England," *Hebrew Union College Annual* 28 (1957), 205–252.

LUND, JOHN. *The Church and the Negro.* N.p., 1967.

McCONKIE, BRUCE R. *Mormon Doctrine.* Salt Lake City, Utah, 1966.

McKEE, D. R. "Isaac de la Peyrère, a Precursor of Eighteenth-Century Critical Deists," *PMLA* 59 (1944), 456–485.

McNAMARA, MARTIN. *The New Testament and the Palestinian Targum to the Pentateuch.* Rome, 1966.

MALAN, S. C., ed. *The Book of Adam and Eve, also called The Conflict of Adam and Eve with Satan.* London, 1882.

MELLINKOFF, RUTH. "Cain's monstrous progeny in *Beowulf*: Part I, Noachic tradition," *Anglo-Saxon England* 8 (1979), 143–162.

―――. "Cain's monstrous progeny in *Beowulf*: Part II, post-diluvian survival," *Anglo-Saxon England* 9 (1980), in press.

―――. *The Horned Moses in Medieval Art and Thought.* Berkeley, Los Angeles, London, 1970.

―――. "The Round-topped Tablets of the Law: Sacred Symbol and Emblem of Evil," *Journal of Jewish Art* 1 (1974), 28–43.

Midrash Tanhuma. New York, Berlin, reprint 1927.

MIGNE, JACQUES PAUL. *Patrologiae cursus completus.* Series Latina, Paris, 1844–1864.

MURDOCH, BRIAN. "An Early Irish Adam and Eve: *Saltair na Rann* and the Traditions of the Fall." *Mediaeval Studies* 35 (1973), 146–177.

New Catholic Encyclopedia. 15 vols. New York, 1967.

New Schaff-Herzog Encyclopedia of Religious Knowledge. 13 vols. New York, London, 1908.

NIEMEYER, G., ed. *Hermannus quondam Judaeus opusculum de conversione sua. Monumenta Germaniae Historica*: Quellen zur Geistesgeschichte des Mittelalters iv. Weimar, 1963.

PÄCHT, OTTO, and J. J. G. ALEXANDER. *Illuminated Manuscripts in the Bodleian Library.* 3 vols. Vol. 3: *British, Irish and Icelandic Schools.* Oxford, 1973.

PAPINI, ROBERTO. *Catalogo delle cose d'arte e di antichità d'Italia.* Ministero della educazione nazionale. Serie I, Fasc. II, parte II. Rome, 1932.

The Pentateuch and Rashi's Commentary, a Linear Translation into English. Translated by Abraham Ben Isaiah and Benjamin Sharfman. Brooklyn, 1949.

Pentateuch with Targum Onkelos, Haphtaroth and Rashi's Commentary. Translated and edited by M. Rosenbaum and A. M. Silbermann. New York, n.d.

PHILLIPS, HENRY E. I. "An Early Stuart Judaising Sect." *The Jewish Historical Society of England (Transactions)* 15 (1939–1945), 63–72.

PHILO. *Questions and Answers on Genesis.* Translated by Ralph Marcus. Loeb Classical Library, Supplement 1. Cambridge, Mass., 1953.

———. *The Worse Attacks the Better.* Translated by F. H. Colson and G. H. Whitaker. Loeb Classical Library. 10 vols. and 2 supplementary vols. Cambridge, Mass. and London, reprint 1968. [1st ed. 1929]

PICKERING, F. P., ed. *The Anglo-Norman Text of the Holk-*

ham *Bible Picture Book*. Anglo-Norman Text Society XXIII. Oxford, 1971.

PRITCHARD, JAMES B. *Solomon and Sheba*. London, 1974.

REISS, EDMUND. "The story of Lamech and its place in medieval drama," *Journal of Medieval and Renaissance Studies* 2 (1972), 35–48.

REVEL-NEHER, ELIZABETH. "Problèmes d'Iconographie Judéo-Chrétienne: Le Thème de la Coiffure du Cohen Gadol dans l'Art Byzantin," *Journal of Jewish Art* 1 (1974), 50–65.

ROTHSCHILD, JAMES DE, ed. *Le Mistère du viel Testament*. 6 vols. Paris, 1878–1891.

RUBENS, ALFRED. *A History of Jewish Costume*. 2d ed. London, 1967 and 1973.

RUNCIMAN, STEVEN. *The Medieval Manichee*. 2d ed. Cambridge, 1960. [1st ed. 1947]

RUPERT OF DEUTZ. *De Sancta Trinitate et Operibus Eius*. Edited by Hrabanus Haacke. *Corpus Christianorum*, vol. 21. Turnhout, 1971.

SALET, FRANCIS. *La Madeleine de Vézelay*. Melun, 1948.

SALTMAN, AVROM. *Pseudo-Jerome, Quaestiones on the Book of Samuel*. Leiden, 1975.

SCHAPIRO, MEYER. "Cain's Jaw-Bone that did the First Murder," *Art Bulletin* 24 (1942), 204–212.

SCHOLEM, GERSHOM. *Kabbalah*. Jerusalem, 1974.

SEMMES, RAPHAEL. *Crime and Punishment in Early Maryland*. Baltimore, 1938.

SMALLEY BERYL. *The Study of the Bible in the Middle Ages*. Oxford, 2d ed. 1952. [1st ed. 1940]

SMITH, JOSEPH. *The Book of Mormon, Doctrine and Covenants*, and *Pearl of Great Price*. Salt Lake City, Utah, 1920. [1st ed. 1830]

SMITH, LUCY TOULMIN, ed. *York Plays: The Plays Performed by the Crafts or Mysteries of York on the Day of Corpus Christi in the 14th, 15th, and 16th Centuries*. Oxford, 1885.

SPERLING, HARRY, and MAURICE SIMON, trans. *The Zohar.* 5 vols. London, Jerusalem, New York, reprint 1973. [1st ed. 1934]

STADE, BERNHARD. "Das Kainszeichen." *Zeitschrift für die alttestamentliche Wissenschaft* 14 (1894), 250–318.

STEFFAN, TRUMAN GUY. *Lord Byron's Cain.* Austin, Texas and London, 1968.

STEPHEN, [SIR] JAMES FITZJAMES. *A History of the Criminal Law of England.* 3 vols. New York, n.d. [1st ed. 1883]

STEWART, JOHN. *Mormonism and the Negro.* Orem, Utah, 1960.

STOKES, WHITLEY, ed. *The Creation of the World [Gwreans an Bys].* Transactions of the Philological Society. 1864.

STRACK, HERMANN L. *Introduction to the Talmud and Midrash.* New York, reprint 1969. [1st ed. 1931]

STRAUS, RAPHAEL. *Die Juden im Königreich Sizilien unter Normannen und Staufern.* Heidelberg, 1910.

THOMPSON, STITH. *Motif-Index of Folk-Literature.* A Classification of Narrative Elements in Folktales, Ballads, Myths, Fables, Mediaeval Romances, Exempla, Fabliaux, Jest-Books, and Local Legends. 6 vols. Bloomington, Indiana, revised and enlarged ed. 1955–1958. [1st ed. 1932–1936]

THORSLEV, PETER L., JR. *The Byronic Hero.* Minneapolis, 1962.

TRACHTENBERG, JOSHUA. *Jewish Magic and Superstition.* Cleveland, New York, and Philadelphia, reprint 1961. [1st ed., Philadelphia, 1939]

VERMES, GEZA. "The Targumic Versions of Genesis IV 3–16," *The Annual of Leeds University Oriental Society* 3 (1961–1962), 81–114.

WILLIAM OF NEWBURGH. *The First Four Books of the "Historia Rerum Anglicarum" (Chronicles of the Reigns of Stephen, Henry II, and Richard I).* Edited by Richard Howlett. 4 vols. London, 1884.

WOODBURY, NAOMI FELICIA. *A Legacy of Intolerance: Nineteenth Century Pro-Slavery Propaganda and the Mormon Church Today.* Master's thesis, University of California at Los Angeles, 1966.

WORMALD, FRANCIS. *The Winchester Psalter.* London, 1973.

Index

Aaron, 26

Abel: portrayal of character of, in the Wakefield *Mactacio Abel,* 82; seen as prototype of Christians, 92–93. *See also* Cain and Abel story

Adambook: Ethiopian, 45–46, 117n76; Irish, 73–74, 100. *See also* Adambooks, Armenian

Adambooks, Armenian: 100, 101; Cain portrayed with horn or horns that speak, 63–65; horn motif combined with Lamech legend, 72–73; Cain described as blackened, 77

Ahasuerus, 38. *See also* Wandering Jew

Albigensians, branding and killing of, 110n6

Alcuin, on the mark of Cain and Cain as city builder, 47

Ambrose, 14, 19, 99; *De Cain et Abel,* 15; on Cain's fears, 15; on the mark of Cain, 15–16; on Cain's punishments, 40–41; Cain compared with Jews and Abel with Christians by, 92–93

American colonies, branding of slaves in, 23

Angelomus of Luxeuil, on Cain as the first city builder, 47

Aramaic: spoken by Jews in Near East, 5–6; versions of Hebrew Bible in (*see* Targum texts)

Augustine of Hippo, 14, 19; allegorical comparison of Cain and the Jews, 17, 41, 92–93, 98; lack of concrete detail on the mark of Cain, 17, 92; on Cain's trembling and groaning, 41; on the mark of Cain, 93–94; and later medieval badge laws for Jews, 98

Aurora, 50, 95–96

Autun. *See* Vézelay and Autun

Badges: required for Jews in medieval times, 97–98, 131n18; Jews punished in Sicily for not wearing, 110n10

Baring-Gould, S., on the mark of Cain, 127n182

Basil the Great, 99; views on sign of Cain, 14, 17–18, 41, 43, 44; on the punishments of Cain, 18, 41, 43, 44

Bayle, Pierre, *Dictionnaire historique et critique:* and the idea of a cross on Cain's forehead, 39–40; on Cain's trembling, 57; on interpretations of the mark of Cain, 121n111

Compositor:	Interactive Composition Corporation
Printer:	Thomson-Shore, Inc.
Text:	VIP Bembo
Cloth:	Holliston Roxite B 53503
Paper:	60 lb. P & S Laid Offset

Plates

1. "Cain and Abel story in five scenes." English Bohun Psalter, ca. A.D. 1370. Oxford Bodleian Library MS. Auct. D.4.4., folio 40. Photo: Courtesy of the Bodleian Library.

2. "God marking Cain." Detail of *fig. 1.*

3. "Cain and Abel scenes." Fresco decoration of the Camposanto at Pisa, A.D. 1390. Photo: Alinari.

4. "God marking Cain." Detail of *fig. 3*.

5. "The Wandering Jew." Color woodcut by Gustave Doré, 1852. Photo: After Eduard Fuchs, *Die Juden in der Karikatur,* Munich, 1921.

6. Detail of *fig. 5.*

first

9. "Death of Cain." Capital from cathedral at Autun, France, half of twelfth century. Photo: Belzeaux–Zodiaque.

10. Detail of *fig. 9.*

7. "Death of Cain." Capital in the nave at Vézelay, France, A.D. 1120. Photo: Claude Bousquet.

8. Detail of capital at Vézelay. Photo: Claude Bousquet.

11. "Death of Cain." Anglo-Norman Bible, England, ca. A.D. 1330. British Library Add. MS. 47682, folio 6 verso. Photo: Courtesy of the Trustees of the British Library.

12. "Cain about to be shot." Detail of *fig. 11.*

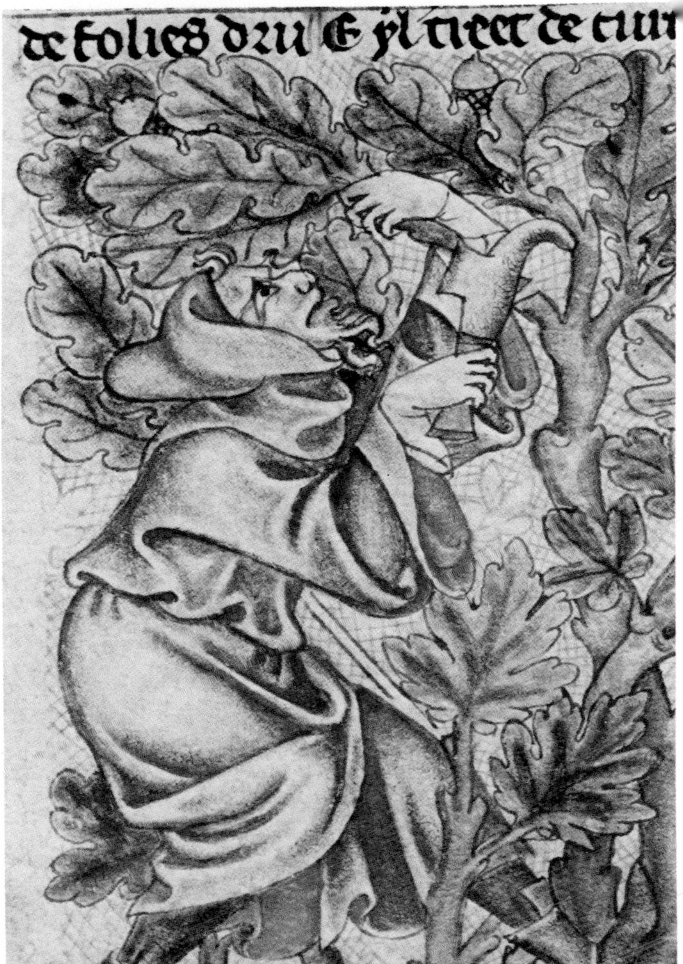

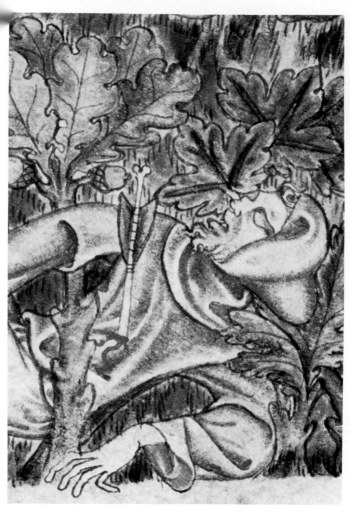

13. "Dead Cain." Detail of *fig. 11.*

14. "Lamech and the youth," and "Youth finding dead Cain."
[Lower scene: Noah and the ark]. Anglo-Norman Bible,
England, ca. A.D. 1330. British Library Add. MS 47682,
folio 7. Photo: Courtesy of the Trustees of the British
Library.

15. "Cain cursed and exiled." Pamplona Bible. Navarra, Spain, ca. A.D. 1194–1234. Collection of Prince Oettingen-Wallerstein, Harburg MS. 1, 2, lat. 4°, 15, folio 6 verso (detail). Photo: Hirsch.

16. "Cain killing Abel." Woodcut by Gerhard Marcks, 1960. Photo: Courtesy of the University of California at Los Angeles Art Gallery.

17. "Cain and Abel bring offerings." English thirteenth-century
psalter. Cambridge, St. John's College Library MS. K. 26,
folio 5 verso. Photo: Courtesy of St. John's College Library.

18. "Cain killing Abel." English thirteenth-century psalter. Cambridge, St. John's College Library MS. K. 26, folio 6. Photo: Courtesy of St. John's College Library.

19. "God cursing and marking Cain." English thirteenth-century
psalter. Cambridge, St. John's College Library MS. K. 26,
folio 6 verso. Photo: Courtesy of St. John's College Library.

20. Detail of *fig. 19.*

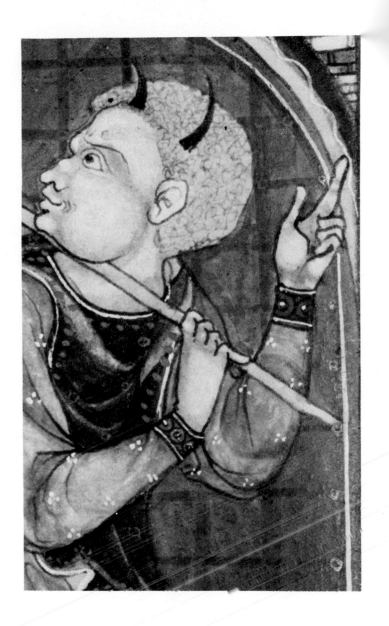

21. "Betrayal and arrest of Christ." English thirteenth-century psalter. Cambridge, St. John's College Library MS. K. 26, folio 18 verso. Photo: Courtesy of St. John's College Library.

22. Detail of *fig. 21*.